TOUCH TYPING
MADE SIMPLE

TOUCH TYPING MADE SIMPLE

Lillian S. Marks

Illustrated by Phillip Jones

A Made Simple Book
Broadway Books
New York

The Library of Congress Cataloging-in-Publication Data has cataloged the Doubleday edition as:
Marks, Lillian S.
Touch Typing Made Simple.
1. Typewriting.   I. Title.
Z49.M34 1985   652.3   85-4431
ISBN 0-385-19426-9

24 23 22 21 20 19 18 17 16 15

CONTENTS

INTRODUCTION

Why learn touch typing? So that your fingers will automatically type accurately and rapidly while your eyes and mind are free to concentrate on the material you are typing.

This book will teach you to master the keyboard in orderly, step-by-step, easy to follow lessons with instructions for electric, electronic, and manual typewriters. Even if you plan to operate a word processor or computer, you should first learn touch typing, since the central keyboard of these machines is basically the same as the typewriter keyboard. You will build speed with each lesson while avoiding the common typing errors associated with traditional methods of instruction. The method of instruction and the sequence of lessons in this book have been perfected while I successfully taught over ten thousand students in New York City high schools.

After you learn how to touch-typewrite with ease, this book will teach you how to build greater speed, set up personal and business letters, address envelopes, make carbon copies, set up tabulations, type on printed forms, divide words at the end of a line, type chemical formulas and mathematical equations, and make changes or corrections on typed copy using an electric, electronic, or manual typewriter.

Touch typing is an important skill. You may wish to acquire it for personal or office use. It is invaluable for a writer, an editor, a lawyer, an executive, and a student. It is a necessity for a typist, a secretary, and any office worker.

You will be well rewarded for the time you spend with this book and your typewriter.

PREPARATION FOR TYPING

The physical action of typing is one that can be easily learned. If you play the piano or any musical instrument on which you depress keys or strings individually, you already know a basic technique of touch typing.

If not, it helps to exercise the fingers of both hands by pretending to play a piano. You must learn to move each finger separately. This can even be done while watching television, five minutes at a time. Repeat until you can depress each finger without moving others.

Electric, Electronic, and Manual Typewriters

The quick slight depressing of the key on an electric or electronic machine activates the electrical impulse that prints the letters. Thus all impressions will be even, no matter whether the type is at the end of a bar (as in most electric typewriters), or on a ball (as in IBM or Xerox), or on a print wheel (as in most electronic typewriters).

On a manual typewriter, the force of your finger sharply striking the key causes the type to hit the ribbon which is in front of the paper. **For even impressions, each finger must hit the key with the same force.**

Typing is faster on an electric or electronic typewriter than on a manual. Since there are more electric and electronic typewriters manufactured than manual, the emphasis in this book will be on the former. However, at each point of difference, the operation of the manual typewriter will be described. The alphabet and the numbers on the keyboard are the same for all types. The location of a few symbols are different on the manual. The electric and electronic machines also have a few additional symbols.

Electronic typewriters have many sophisticated features that you should not be concerned about until *after* you have mastered touch typing of the keyboard.

Do not use the correction devices until you can type accurately and speedily. To use them before you are ready will slow the learning process.

An electronic typewriter has a memory, from ten letters to many lines, depending on the machine. If your fingers type faster than the machine prints, the machine will catch up.

For effective learning, set aside a definite period of time every day to practice typewriting until you master the keyboard. If there are days when this is not possible, typewrite for at least fifteen minutes, so that your fingers do not lose their facility.

TOUCH TYPING
MADE SIMPLE

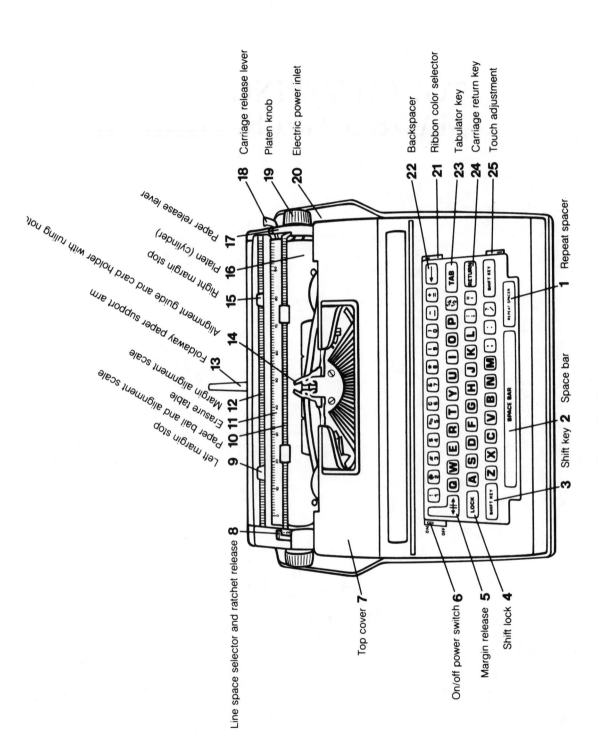

Fig. 1 The Electric Typewriter

18 Carriage release lever
19 Platen knob
20 Electric power inlet

22 Backspacer
21 Ribbon color selector
23 Tabulator key
24 Carriage return key
25 Touch adjustment

17 Paper release lever
16 Platen (cylinder)
15 Right margin stop
14 Alignment guide and card holder with ruling not.
13 Foldaway paper support arm
12 Margin alignment scale
11 Erasure table
10 Paper ball and alignment scale
9 Left margin stop

8 Line space selector and ratchet release

7 Top cover
6 On/off power switch
5 Margin release
4 Shift lock

3 Shift key
2 Space bar
1 Repeat spacer

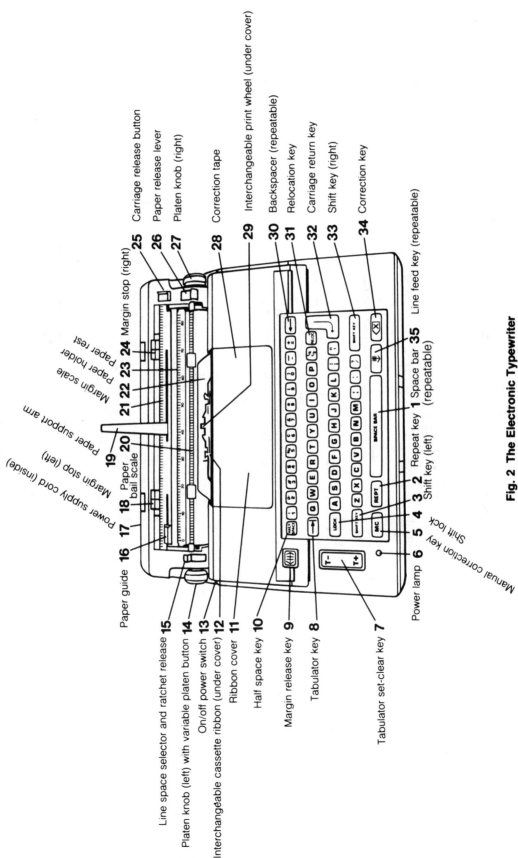

Paper guide **16**
Line space selector and ratchet release **15**
Platen knob (left) with variable platen button **14**
On/off power switch **13**
Interchangeable cassette ribbon (under cover) **12**
Ribbon cover **11**

Half space key **10**

Margin release key **9**

Tabulator key **8**

Tabulator set-clear key **7**

Power lamp **6**

Power supply cord (inside) **17**
Margin stop (left) **18**
Paper bail scale **19**
Paper support arm **20**
Margin scale **21**
Paper holder **22**
Paper rest **23**
Margin stop (right) **24**

25 Carriage release button
26 Paper release lever
27 Platen knob (right)

28 Correction tape

29 Interchangeable print wheel (under cover)
30 Backspacer (repeatable)
31 Relocation key
32 Carriage return key
33 Shift key (right)

34 Correction key

Repeat key **1** Space bar **1**
(repeatable)
Shift key (left) **2**
3 REPT
4
Shift lock **5**
Manual correction key
35 Line feed key (repeatable)

Fig. 2 The Electronic Typewriter

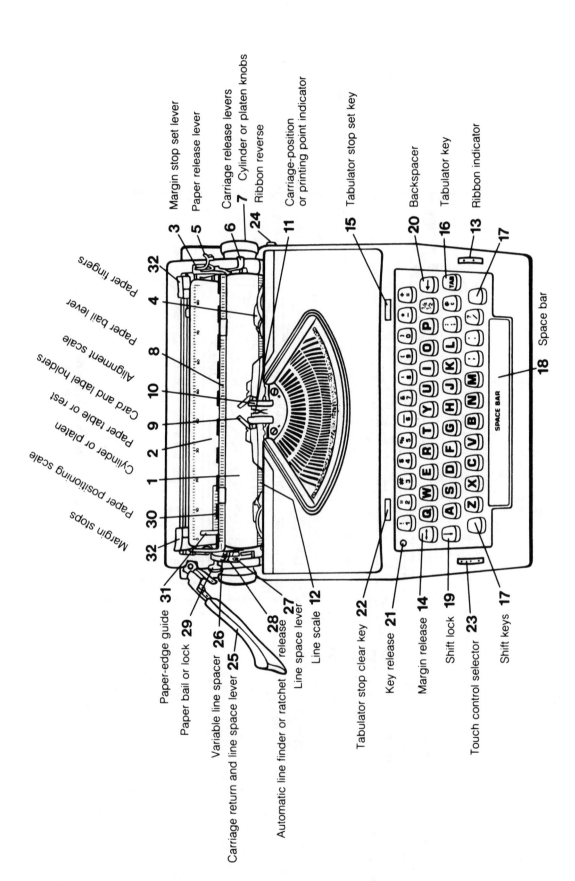

Margin stop set lever **3**
Paper release lever **5**
Carriage release levers **6**
Cylinder or platen knobs **7**
Ribbon reverse **24**
Carriage-position or printing point indicator **11**
Tabulator stop set key **15**
Backspacer **20**
Tabulator key **16**
Ribbon indicator **13**
17

Paper fingers **32**
4
Paper bail lever **8**
Alignment scale
Card and label holders **10**
Paper table or rest **9**
Cylinder or platen **2**
Paper positioning scale **1**
Margin stops **30**
32

Paper-edge guide **31**
Paper bail or lock **29**
Variable line spacer **26**
Carriage return and line space lever **25**
Automatic line finder or ratchet release **28**
Line space lever **27**
Line scale **12**
Tabulator stop clear key **22**
Key release **21**
Margin release **14**
Shift lock **19**
Touch control selector **23**
Shift keys **17**

Space bar **18**

SPACE BAR

Fig. 3 The Manual Typewriter

LESSON 1

Aim: To learn
1. Major parts of the machine
2. To set margins
3. The **guide-key** position
4. Keys **A S D F ;**

Preparing to Type

Place this book to the right of the typewriter. Check to see that the cord of your electric or electronic typewriter is connected to an electric outlet. Turn the control switch on. Since machines differ, you may find this switch on the right side of your keyboard, the left side of the keyboard, or even the back of the machine.

If you cannot locate any part of the machine in the area described in this text, consult the instruction manual that accompanies your machine for its location on your machine.

Adjust the Paper Guide at 0
The paper guide is a strip of metal above the left end of the cylinder. Slide the paper guide until its vertical edge points to 0 on the scale. (See Fig. 4.)

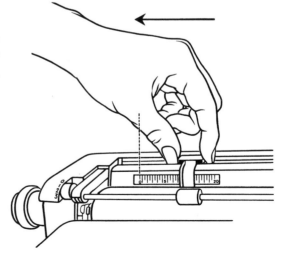

Fig. 4 Adjusting the paper guide at 0

1

Insert the Paper

Hold the paper with the thumb and four fingers of your left hand.

Place the paper squarely behind the cylinder, left edge against the paper guide.

Place your thumb under the right cylinder knob and the first two fingers on top.

Vigorously spin the knob away from you. (See Fig. 5.)

Fig. 5 Inserting the paper

Adjust the Paper Bail

Place the paper bail over the paper and move the small rollers so that they are equidistant from the edges of the paper. (See Fig. 6.)

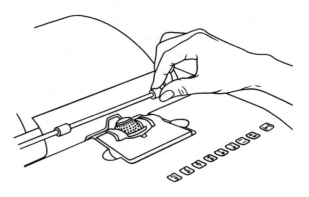

Fig. 6 Adjusting the paper bail and the small rollers

Straighten the Paper

Your paper is straight if the left edge of the front part is even with the left edge of the back part—and both at the paper guide.

If your paper is not straight, lift the paper bail, depress the paper release (near the right knob), and straighten the paper. Holding the paper in place with your left hand, push the paper release back to position with your right hand.   (See Fig. 7.)

Remove the Paper

Depress the **paper release** with your right hand and draw the paper out with your left hand.   Return the **paper release** to position.   Practice inserting and removing the paper, finally leaving the paper in the machine.

Fig. 7 Straightening the paper

Setting the Line Space Gauge

The line space gauge is an indicator at the left end of the cylinder. (On the IBM it is above the right cylinder.) The line space gauge regulates the spacing between lines—single, 1½, double, and on some machines triple. Adjust the indicator to "1" for single spacing. (See Fig. 8.)

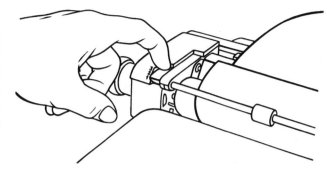

Fig. 8 Line space gauge at 1

Center the Carrier

If your machine has a **movable carriage** (the part that holds the cylinder), you can center it by depressing the **carriage release** (the spring which is above the right-hand knob). Hold on to the knob as you depress the carriage release and move the carriage to the center. (See Fig. 9.) Remove your hand from the carriage release.

If you machine has a **movable print ball** or **movable daisy wheel,** strike the RETURN key by tapping it once with your right pinkie. (It may be marked RETURN or it may bear an arrow symbol.) The RETURN key brings the printing element to a new line at the left margin. Since you want the carrier to be in the center, press the **space bar** with your right thumb. Your space bar has a repeat action. Release it when the printing indicator is at the center.

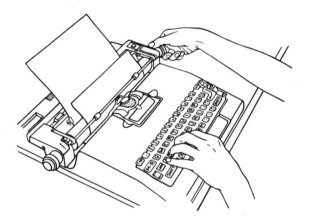

Fig. 9 Centering the carrier

Fig. 10 Some return keys bear this symbol.

Setting the Margin Stops

The margin stops set the points at which the typing line begins and ends.

First note whether your 8½-inch paper (standard business size) measures 85 or 101 across on the paper scale. You may find this scale on the paper bail and/or on the back of the paper rest. If your paper measures 85, the pitch of your machine is 10 spaces to the inch and your type is **pica** (10 spaces × 8½ inches = 85 spaces). If your paper measures 101 or 102, the pitch of your machine is 12 spaces to the inch and your type is **elite** (12 spaces × 8½ inches = 102). If your machine can be adjusted for pica or elite, set it for pica.

For hand setting, the **margin stops** are usually on the back of the paper rest. Depress the stop and slide the stop to the desired position, first the left and then the right. (See Fig. 11.)

For a machine with **automatic margin setting,** depress the **automatic left margin** lever and bring the carrier (carriage or printing point) to the desired left margin. Release the lever. Do the same for the **automatic right margin.** For pica type, set the margins at 15 and 72. For elite type, set the margins at 25 and 82. This will give you a writing line of 55 spaces with a leeway of 2 spaces.

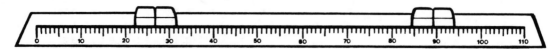

Fig. 11 Scale with margin stops

Top Margin

All typewriters are adjusted to type 6 lines to the inch from top to bottom. You should leave a top margin of 1½ inches (9 lines).

Turn the cylinder knob toward you until the top edge of the paper is level with the typing line.

ELECTRIC AND ELECTRONIC: Tap the RE-TURN key ten times with the right pinkie. By typing on the tenth line from the top edge of the paper, you leave a top margin of 9 blank lines—1½ inches.

MANUAL: Strike the carriage return lever ten times with the left hand. (Hold four fingers of your left hand together, palm down. Strike the lever with the lower section of your first finger, backed up by the others. "Throw" the carriage sharply.) (See Fig. 12.)

Fig. 12 Throwing the carriage

Learning to Type

Correct Typing Posture

Sit erect facing your machine, keeping the center of your body a little to the right of the keyboard. Your lower spine should be at the back of the chair. The distance between you and the typewriter should be 9 or 10 inches. Both feet should be flat on the floor, one foot slightly ahead of the other.

Guide Keys

This is the home position of your fingers while typing:

Place four fingers of **left** hand on **A S D F** (pinkie on **A**)

Place four fingers of **right** hand on **J K L ;** (pinkie on **;**)

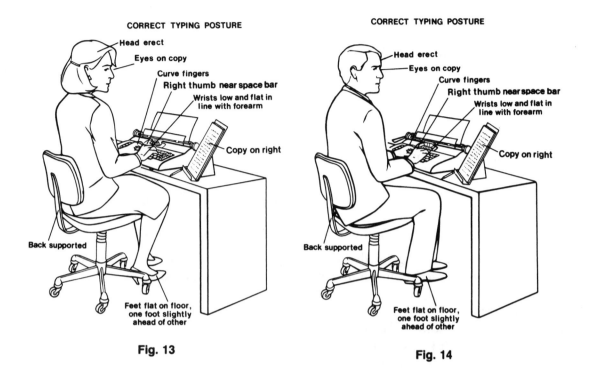

Fig. 13

Fig. 14

Position of Hands

Curving your fingers naturally, let your fingertips rest very lightly on the center of each guide key. You will be striking each key with the ball of your finger. Slant hands upward from the wrists. Keep wrists low but *not* touching the machine. Keep your elbows close to your body. If you are right-handed, let your right thumb drop naturally near the space bar and let your left thumb curl under. If you are left-handed, reverse this. (See Fig. 15.)

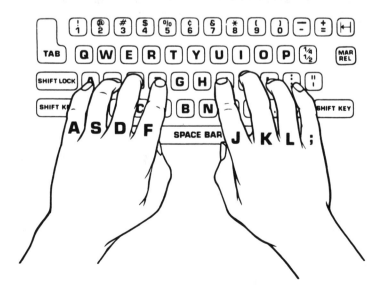

Fig. 15 Fingers on guide keys

How to Typewrite

(REMINDER: This book should be at your right.)

Using the Space Bar

With the side of your thumb, tap the space bar sharply and quickly as many times as it takes until you are stopped by the margin stop.

Practicing the Return Function

In this text, RETURN will mean tapping the return key or throwing the carriage.

ELECTRIC AND ELECTRONIC: Reach for the RETURN key with your right pinkie, lightly holding on to **J K** and **L**. Depress the RETURN key and immediately return the finger to ;. Practice this reach several times without looking at your fingers.

MANUAL: Throw the carriage as described on p. 4. Immediately return the left hand to the guide keys. Practice this until you can do this without looking.

Striking the Keys

ELECTRIC AND ELECTRONIC: Tap each key lightly.
MANUAL: Strike each key sharply with equal force.
After striking, quickly retract the finger. Do not let the finger linger on the depressed key.

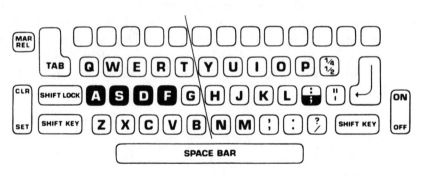

Fig. 16

New Keys A and S

Looking at the keyboard chart, feel the **A** key with the left pinkie. (All eight fingers should be on the guide keys.) Strike the **A** key sharply three times; space; and repeat so that your paper looks like this:

aaa aaa aaa aaa aaa aaa aaa aaa aaa aaa aaa aaa aaa aaa

Feel the **S** key next to **A**. With the **A** finger and **S** finger, type these 2 lines. Say the letters as you type them. (Think of these two fingers as your **A** finger and your **S** finger.)

```
aaa sss aaa sss aaa sss aaa sss aaa sss aaa sss aaa sss
as as as as as as as as as as as as as as as as as as as
```

Self-Testing Work: Test yourself on **A** and **S** and the space bar. At the end of a line after striking the RETURN key, immediately return to ; and continue typing on the new line without looking up.

Do not look at your fingers. Keep your eyes on the book. If you need to verify the location of a key, look at the Keyboard Chart in the book.

Copy these 3 lines exactly. Tap the keys sharply. Say the letters as you type them.

```
as as as as as as as as as as as as as as as as as as as
sass sass sass sass sass sass sass sass sass sass sass
a as sass a as sass a as sass a as sass a as sass a as
```

Were you able to type the 3 lines without looking up from the book?

If you have a manual machine, you should be able to throw the carriage and return your left hand to the guide keys without looking up. If not, practice more.

If you have an error or two, don't be upset. You will soon have complete control of your fingers. Don't stop typing if you feel you have made an error; just keep going; do not strike over an error.

Now stop typing for a moment and relax. Shake your hands loosely from the wrists. *Whenever you stop typing on your electric or electronic machine for more than a few minutes, turn the switch to OFF.*

New Key D

Step 1—New Key Preview

Touch the **A** and **S** keys. Now feel **A** and **S** and **D**. Feel **A S D**.

Step 2—New Key Tryout

Start each line slowly and gradually increase speed. Control your fingers. If you lose control, slow down. Say the letters as you type them. RETURN an extra time after the first two lines.

```
ddd ddd ddd ddd ddd ddd asd asd asd asd asd asd asd asd
add add add add add add add add add add add add add add

adds adds adds adds adds adds adds adds adds adds adds
dad dad dad dad dad dad dad dad dad dad dad dad dad dad
sad sad sad sad sad sad sad sad sad sad sad sad sad sad
```

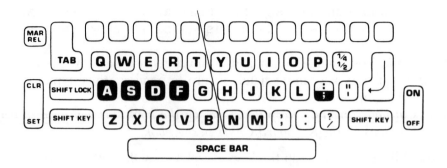

New Key ; (Semicolon)

Step 1—New Key Preview

The fingers of your right hand are covering **J K L ;**. With your right pinkie, feel the key ;.

The semicolon is typed directly after the preceding letter with no space between. However, there is always a space **after** a semicolon (hereafter called semi).

Step 2—New Key Tryout

Typewrite a line of semi, space, semi, space, etc. Remember to say the letters as you type them.

```
; ; ; ; ; ; ; ; ; ; ; ; ; ; ; ; ; ; ; ; ; ; ; ; ;
dad adds; dad adds; dad adds; dad adds; dad adds;
a sad dad; a sad dad; a sad dad; a sad dad; a sad dad;
```

New Key F

Step 1—New Key Preview

With your left hand, feel **A S D**. Now feel **A S D F**.

Step 2—New Key Tryout

```
fff fff fff fff fff fff asdf asdf asdf asdf asdf asdf
aff aff aff aff aff aff aff aff aff aff aff aff aff aff
daff daff daff daff daff daff daff daff daff daff daff

fad fad fad fad fad fad fad fad fad fad fad fad fad fad
fads fads fads fads fads fads fads fads fads fads fads
```

Except for obvious drills, all the combination of letters in this text are words. You may find some new words for your Scrabble game. Look up the definitions in an unabridged dictionary.

Self-Testing Work: You have learned the location of **A S D F ;** and the fingers to which they belong. Never use any other fingers for these letters. Test yourself to see how well you have learned them. Keep your eyes on the copy. If you forget the location of a letter, look at the keyboard chart, not at your fingers. Type the following eight lines. RETURN twice after every second line.

Typing Tip: Say the letters as you type them until your fingers respond automatically to the sight of the letters.

```
aaa sss ddd fff ;;; aaa sss ddd fff ;;; aaa sss ddd fff
a sad dad; a sad dad; a sad dad; a sad dad; a sad dad;

a sad fad; a sad fad; a sad fad; a sad fad; a sad fad;
fad fads; fad fads; fad fads; fad fads; fad fads;

sad fads; sad fads; sad fads; sad fads; sad fads;
as sad as dad; as sad as dad; as sad as dad;

as sad as a fad; as sad as a fad; as sad as a fad;
a sad dad adds; a sad dad adds; a sad dad adds;
```

Now relax for a moment. Shake your hands.

Improvement Work: Type another copy of the above eight lines. See if you can type them more smoothly and more accurately.

To remove paper, press paper release with right hand and remove paper with left hand. Return paper release to its original position. *Turn switch off.*

In this lesson you have learned to use a semicolon. Its proper use denotes a separation in a sentence that is greater than a comma but less than a period. However, until you learn the keys for a comma, a period, and a question mark, the semicolon will be used in their place.

Here's a tip to help you improve your typing when you are away from the typewriter: As you walk in the street, ride in a bus, or wait for an appointment, think of the words you have just learned and move your fingers as if to respond to the feel of the letters.

LESSON 2

Aim: To learn keys **L K J E**

Machine Adjustments
1. Paper guide: at 0
2. Line space gauge: single spacing
3. Margin stops: 15 (25) and 72 (82)
   Elite is in parentheses.
4. Top margin: 1½ inches (type on tenth line from top edge)

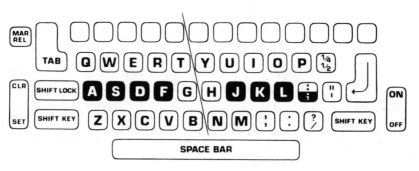

Fig. 17

Warm-up (5 minutes):

Set a timer if you have one. Type the following 4 lines exactly. If you finish them ahead of time, type them again. Keep your eyes on the book. If you must look for a letter, look at the chart, not at your fingers. Say the letters to yourself as you type them. By looking at the copy, you can surely see that you should RETURN twice after the second line.

```
aaa sss ddd fff ;;; aaa sss ddd fff ;;; aaa sss ddd fff
as as as as; add add add add; dad dad dad dad; sad sad

fad fad fad fad; fads fads fads fads; adds adds adds;
dad adds; dad adds; a sad fad; a sad fad; a sad fad;
```

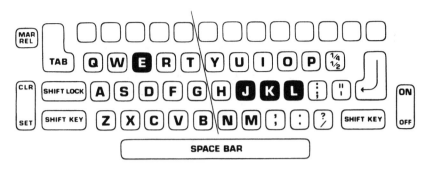

Fig. 18

New Key L

Step 1—New Key Preview

Place eight fingers on the guide keys. Look at the chart and with your right hand, feel keys **J K L ;**. Now feel **; L**.

Step 2—New Key Tryout

To strike **L**, hold on to **J** and **K** lightly. Lift the **L** finger and tap the key sharply with your fingertip. Type the following 12 lines, saying the letters. Increase speed as you keep control:

```
lll ;;; lll ;;; lll ;;; lll ;;; lll ;;; lll ;;; lll ;;;
all all all all all all all all all all all all all all

fall fall fall fall fall fall fall fall fall fall fall
falls falls falls falls falls falls falls falls falls

lad lad lad lad lad lad lad lad lad lad lad lad lad lad
lass lass lass lass lass lass lass lass lass lass lass

sal sal sal sal sal sal; salad salad salad salad salad;
alas alas alas alas alas alas; lads lads lads lads lads

a sad salad; a sad salad; a sad salad; a sad salad;
a lass falls; a lass falls; all lads fall; all lads fall;

dad falls; dad falls; dad falls; dad falls; dad falls;
alas a sad lad falls; alas a sad lad falls; a sad lad;
```

New Keys J and K

Step 1—New Key Preview

With your right hand, feel keys **J K L ;**. Feel **; L K J**. Now feel **J K**.

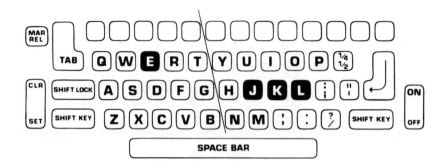

Step 2—New Key Tryout

To strike **J**: Let your finger touch **;** **L** **K** lightly. Now lift your **J** finger and tap **J** sharply with your fingertip.

To strike **K**: Let your fingers touch **;** and **L** lightly. With your **K** finger tap **K** sharply. Say the letters as you type.

```
jjj kkk jjj kkk jjj kkk jjj kkk jjj kkk jjj kkk jjj kkk
jak jak jak jak jak jak jak jak jak jak jak jak jak jak

jad jad jad jad jad jad jad jad jad jad jad jad jad jad
ask ask ask ask ask ask; flask flask flask flask flask

asks asks asks asks asks; akala akala akala akala akala
kas kas kas kas kas kas; flak flak flak flak flak flak

ask dad; a lad asks dad; ask dad; a lad asks dad;
a lad asks a lass; a lass asks dad; a lad asks a lass
```

New Key E

Step 1—New Key Preview

Try to pretend that the fingers are attached to the guide keys with rubber bands. Each finger of the guide keys types other letters on the keyboard, but the finger is quickly returned to its guide key. Since you know your guide keys, you will now learn which letters each finger controls.

The **D** finger always controls **E**. Look at the chart. Touching **A** and **S**, lift your **D** finger to the line above, slightly to the left. You are now touching **E**. Feel **D E D** several times as you say **D E D**. Remember to return to **D** after striking **E**.

At the end of each word, all fingers should be on the guide keys.

Step 2—New Key Tryout

```
ded ded ded ded ded ded ded ded ded ded ded ded ded ded
deed deed deed deed; seed seed seed seed; feed feed feed

dead dead dead dead; lead lead lead lead; self self self
led led led; sled sled sled; fed fed fed; fled fled fled
```

```
jade jade jade jade; fade fade fade fade; jess jess jess
desk desk desk desk; keds keds keds keds; seek seek seek

eel eel eel eel; feel feel feel feel; keel keel keel
sell sell sell; fell fell fell; jell jell jell jell jell
```

Self-Testing Work: Test your mastery of all the guide keys plus **E**. Type the following 12 lines. Don't rush, but tap the keys sharply. Don't look at your fingers. Think of the finger and key or keys it controls. With sufficient practice, your finger should respond to the sight of the letter it controls.

```
deal deal deal; seal seal seal; eke eke eke; seek seek
lake lake lake; sake sake sake; slake slake slake; fake

else else else; less less less; ale ale ale; dale dale
sale sale sale; kale kale kale; leek leek leek; sleek

fee fee fee; see see see; sea sea sea; lea lea lea; leak
lease lease lease; deaf deaf deaf; leaf leaf leaf; self

jade jade jade; ease ease ease; easel easel easel; jell
jell eels; jell eels; jell eels; jell eels; jell eels;

feel safe; sell jade; feel safe; sell jade; feel safe;
seal a deal; seal a leak; seal a deal; seal a flask;

seek a safe lake; seek a safe lake; seek a safe lake;
lease a desk; lease a desk; lease a desk; lease a desk;
```

Corrective Work:
1. Proofread by comparing your work carefully with the copy, word for word.
2. Circle the words which are incorrect: typographical error, wrong word, additional word; indicate an omitted word.
3. Write a list of the corrected words on a separate sheet of paper.
4. Practice these words by typewriting each one five times correctly.

NOTE: A warning bell rings when the carrier is 6 or 7 spaces from the right margin. Test your machine to determine how many spaces before the margin stop your bell rings.

When you hear the bell, finish the word you are typing and RETURN for a new line.

TYPING TIP: If you have written a wrong word, an additional word, or omitted a word, it is the result of taking your eyes away from your copy while typing. Remedy it!

Now relax for a moment. If you feel tense, stand up and stretch.

To improve, type the Self-Testing Work Again. See if you can type it more smoothly and more accurately.

LESSON 3

Aim: To learn keys **I R T G**

Machine Adjustments:
1. Always check that paper guide is at 0. This instruction will not be repeated.
2. Spacing will be indicated before the first exercise of each lesson. Change the spacing only when indicated.
3. Margins will be noted for pica at the left and right. The numbers in parentheses are the elite margins.

Single spacing

15 (25)   72 (82)

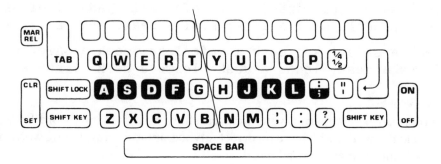

Warm-up (5 minutes): Always say the letters of the drill as you type it. Say the letters of the words if you find it helpful. If you finish before the five minutes are up, start again.

> TYPING TIP: Tap the keys with a staccato touch. Return fingers quickly to guide keys.

```
asdf jkl; ded asdf jkl; ded asdf jkl; ded asdf jkl; ded
deed feed seed; led sled fed fled; fake lake sake slake;

fade faded; jade jaded; lade laded; slaked faked; desk
eels feels keels; deals seals; jell jells jelled; ladle

safe seals; a jade flask; a faded leaf; a sad sale;
dad sells desks; a lad sells seeds; a lass feeds a seal;
```

14

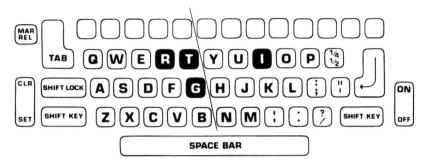

Fig. 19

New Key I

Step 1—New Key Preview

I is controlled by the **K** finger. With the fingers of your right hand, lightly touch ; and **L**. Lift the **K** finger and reach up and slightly to the left. You are touching **I**. Look at the chart, not at your fingers. Feel **K I K** until you are familiar with the reach. Then return fingers to guide keys.

Step 2—New Key Tryout

```
kik kik kik kik kik kik kik kik kik kik kik kik kik kik
kiss kiss kiss; kill kill kill; skill skill skill;

silk silk silk; ail ail ail; sail sail sail; fail fail
jail jail jail; like like like; dislike dislike dislike

dike dike dike; fill fill fill; sill sill sill; dill
die die die; side side side; kid kid kid; skid skid skid

kief kief kief; aid aid aid; said said said; laid laid
dais dais dais; dial dial dial; slide slide slide;

dad dials; dad dials; dad dials; dad dials; dad dials;
a lad dislikes jail; a kid slides; a silk sail fails;
```

New Keys R T G

Step 1—New Key Preview

R T and **G** are all controlled by the **F** finger. Move *only* the **F** finger for striking these keys. With **F** finger, reach up and slightly to the left for **R**. Feel **F R F** several times while looking at the chart. Say **F R F** as you feel for this reach.

For **T** reach up and to the right. Feel **F T F** several times. Feel **T**. Feel **F R T F**. Feel **F R F T F**. Feel **R** and **T**. Repeat these reaches as you say the letters.

For **G** again move only the **F** finger. Look at the chart and feel **G** to the right. Feel **F G F** several times. Feel **R T G**. Be sure to return to **F**.

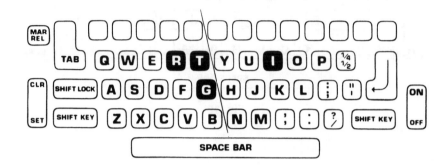

Step 2—New Key Tryout

Say the drills.

```
frf frf frf ftf ftf ftf fgf fgf fgf frftfgf frftfgf
frtf frtf frtf frtgf frtgf frf ftf fgf frf ftf fgf

far far far far far far far far far far far far far far
fat fat fat fat fat fat fat fat fat fat fat fat fat fat
gaff gaff gaff gaff gaff gaff gaff gaff gaff gaff gaff

raft raft raft; graft graft graft; rift rift rift;
drift drift drift; sift sift sift; gift gift gift;

sag lag flag rag drag jag tag; sag lag flag rag jag tag;
eat seat feat great; get let set jet; eat seat feat;

fig dig jig gig; fig dig jig gig; leg keg; legs kegs
ear fear tear dear gear rear sear lear; art start tart

did all lads register; did all lads register; register
it is a gift; it is a gift; it is a gift; a great gift;
```

Self-Testing Work

Test your mastery of the new keys **I R T G**. Copy these lines exactly.

REMINDER: Your fingers should be back at the guide keys at the end of every word.

```
fired fired fired; tired tired tired; tried tried tried;
fast fast fast; first first first; tariff tariff tariff;

fir fit fig; fir fit fig; fir fit fig; fir fit fig;
gift lift sift rift drift; gift lift sift rift drift;

aft daft draft graft raft; sit lit fit kit skit frit;
ate fate rate gate late date state slate skate grate
```

```
get a garage; it is late; a large staff; a first date;
a dark street; a great treat; a late date; a tired kid;

address letters; file letters; letters are filed first;
a fair trial; a fast retreat; a first feast; a dark jail

get gas at a garage; it is fragile if it is glass;
take a diet dessert; stage a strike; settle strikes;

free trade; grass seed; ideal ideas; take a little test
sit at a desk; grade all tests; a free treat at last;
```

Corrective Work: Make a list of the words in which you find errors. Practice each word correctly five times.

Now relax. Shake your hands. Stand up and stretch. If you are very tired, check your typing position with the description in Lesson 1. Proper typing position prevents fatigue.

Improvement Work: Type the above 14 lines again. You should be able to type them more easily and more accurately.

LESSON 4

Aim: To learn keys **W U Y H**

Typing Tip for **electronic** machines only: Some electronic machines have a slow carrier RETURN. If you are ready to type on the next line before the machine stops, you may start typing immediately. An electronic typewriter has a memory and will print the letters you struck as soon as the next line is reached. It will catch up with you.

15 (25)

72 (82)

Single spacing

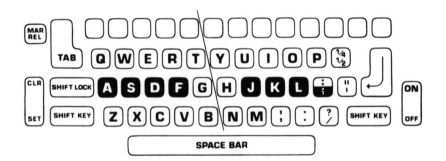

Warm-up (5 minutes):

Copy the first two lines while saying the drills. RETURN twice and type the next line ten times. This line reviews all the letters you have learned.

```
asdf jkl; asdf jkl; ded frf ftf fgf kik ded frf ftf fgf
kik ded frf ftf fgf kik ded frf ftf fgf kik ded frf ftf

a jagged edge; ask if it is a glass jar; file a letter
```

New Key W

Step 1—New Key Preview

The **S** finger controls **W**. On the chart, note that **W** is above **S**, slightly to the left. Lightly touching **D** and **F**, reach with the **S** finger for **W**. Feel **S W S** until you are comfortable with the reach. Memorize **S W S**.

18

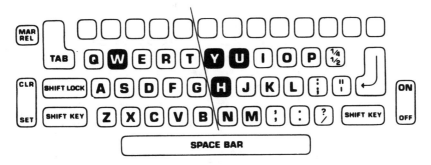

Fig. 20

Step 2—New Key Tryout

```
sws sws sws sws sws sws sws sws sws sws sws sws sws sws
saw saw saw saw; was was was was; waste waste waste waste

swell swell swell; sweet sweet sweet; west west west;
raw raw raw; straw straw straw; jaw jaw jaw; jaws jaws;

sew sew sew; stew stew stew; grew grew grew; few few few
wear wear wear; swear swear swear; wrist wrist wrist;

jewel jewel jewel; sweater sweater sweater; will will
saw raw jaw law daw; wet wed well were wedge weak weeds;

wet water; wise laws; we saw a few large jewels;
we will wear sweaters; we will write a few letters;
```

New Keys U Y H

Step 1—New Key Preview

The **J** finger controls **U Y** and **H**. Looking at the chart, reach up with the **J** finger, slightly to the left for **U**. Feel **J U J** several times. Move only the **J** finger.

Now feel **U**, and still anchored at **; L K** with your other fingers, feel to the left of **U** for **Y**. Feel **J U Y J**. Feel **J U J J Y J**. Feel **J Y J** several times until you can reach **Y** comfortably. Feel **U** and feel **Y**.

Holding on to **; L K**, reach with the **J** finger to the left for **H**. Feel **J H J** several times.

Feel **U Y H**.

The imaginary rubber band should always bring the **J** finger back to its home key. However, if you need to type **HU** or **YU**, it is not necessary to touch **J** between these letters provided that you are back on the guide key by the end of the word.

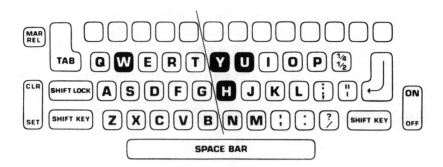

Step 2—New Key Tryout

Say the drills.

```
juj juj juj juj juj juj juj juyj juyj juyj juyj juyj
juj jyj juj jyj juj jyj juj jyj juj jyj juj jyj juj

jhj jhj jhj jhj jhj jhj jhj juj jyj jhj juj jyj jhj
jujyjhj jujyjhj jujyjhj jujyjhj jujyjhj jujyjhj jujyjhj

just just just; jug jug jug; jugular jugular jugular;
us us us; use use use; usual usual usual; judge judge;

jay jay jay; jury jury jury; truly truly truly; day day
yes yes yes; yesterday yesterday yesterday; yell yell

key key key; usually usually usually; urge urge urge;
day say lay gray tray jay fray stay stray flay ray gay;

hajj hajj hajj hajj hajj hajj hajj hajj hajj hajj hajj
hall hall hall; shall shall shall; hull hull hull;

hurry hurry hurry; hush hush hush; fish fish fish;
fresh fresh fresh; had had had; half half half; has has

why why why; where where where; what what what; while
the the the; these these these; they they they; this

laugh laughter taught daughter fight light height sight
hue huff hug huge hulk hush hurdle hurrah hurt hydra
fly sly try dry rye slay lay jay hay way sway dray shay
```

Self-Testing Work
See how well you have trained your fingers to locate the new keys in this lesson.

Do not strike one letter over another.
Don't worry about errors.
Keep your eyes on this page.
Finish every line you start.

```
saw saw saw; was was was; wash wash wash; wish wish wish
laws laws laws; lawsuit lawsuit lawsuit; with with with

just justly judge jury; hurry hurry hurry; we were; were
why why why; guy guy guy; try try try; guru guru guru;

yes yes yes; yesterday yesterday yesterday; day day day
trust trust trust; true true true; truly truly truly

while while while; where where where; whisk whisk whisk
high high high; sigh sigh sigh; height height height;

weight weight weight; right right right; tight tight;
lightly slightly rightly; lightly slightly rightly;

he likes fruit; she saw a far star; she wears a garter;
a guru taught her; a guru taught her; a guru taught;
he has a huge shag rug; it is a large high grade rug;

what was the weather like yesterday at the fair;
ask her whether she will stay with us while she is here;

a law; a just law; a truly just law; a law that is just;
the judge usually judges us justly; the judge judges us;

the jury is ready; the trial is fair; a fair result;
he trusts the jury; she trusts the judge; they trust;
```

Corrective Work: Check your work carefully. List the words in which you find errors. Practice each word correctly five times.

RELAX

Improvement Work: Type the 19 lines again. Try for ease and accuracy.

Do your fingers feel for the new words when you are away from the typewriter?

LESSON 5

Aim: To learn keys **O P Q Z**

15 (25)

72 (82)
Single spacing

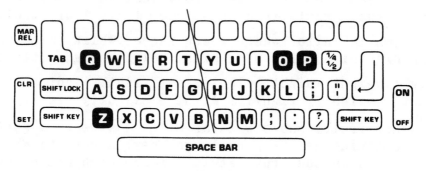

Fig. 21

Warm-up (5 minutes):

After the drill, type the next line ten times. (Say the drill as you type it.)

```
asdf jkl; sws ded frf ftf fgf juj jyj jhj kik fgf jhj
asdf jkl; sws ded frf ftf fgf juj jyj jhj kik fgf jhj

they asked us if we will just try to get there early;
```

New Keys O and P

O is controlled by the **L** finger.

P is controlled by the ; finger (the pinkie).

Step 1—New Key Preview

Lightly holding on to **J** and **K**, feel with the **L** finger up and slightly to the left for **O**. Look at the chart and feel **L O L**. Feel **L O L** several times. Feel **O**.

Lightly holding on to **J K L**, feel **P** with the semi finger. Feel ; **P** ; several times. Feel **P**.

Feel **L O L** ; **P** ;. Feel **O**. Feel **P**. Repeat.

Step 2—New Key Tryout

REMINDER: Keep your elbows close to your sides.   Keep your eyes on the book.

```
lol lol lol lol lol lol lol lol ;p; ;p; ;p; ;p; ;p; ;p;
lol ;p; lol ;p; lol ;p; lol ;p; lol ;p; lol ;p; lol ;p;

look look look; loss loss loss; load load load; loaf
old old old; sold sold sold; fold fold fold; gold gold

pal pal pal; poll poll poll; pool pool pool; poke poke
pay pay pay; hope hope hope; lap lap lap; lip lip lip;

please please please; pleasure pleasure pleasure; pot
joke joke joke; happy happy happy; party party party;

to to to; for for for; four four four; pour pour pour;
you you you; your your your; past past past; post post

we are pleased to go to your party; we are happy to go;
we hope to sell our house for a profit this year;
```

New Keys Q and Z
The **A** finger controls both **A** and **Z**.
Q is the last letter to be learned on the line above the guide keys.
Z is the first letter to be learned on the line below the guide keys.
The same finger strikes the first and last letters in the alphabet, **A** and **Z**.

Step 1—New Key Preview

Lightly touching **S D F**, reach up and to the left with your **A** finger for **Q**. Look at the chart and feel **A Q A** until you memorize it.

For **Z**, feel down to the line below, slightly to the right.   Feel **A Z A** until you are comfortable with the reach.   Feel **A Q A   A Z A**. Feel **Q**. Feel **Z**.

Step 2—New Key Tryout

```
aqa aqa aqa aqa aqa aqa aqa aqa; aza aza aza aza aza aza
aqua aqua aqua; azure azure azure azure; aqua aqua aqua

quart quart quart; quality quality quality; qualify
queer queer queer; request request request; require

zeal zeal zeal; zealous zealous zealous; lazy lazy lazy
quartz quartz quartz; azalea azalea azalea; zest zest

quoted quoted quoted; equipped equipped equipped; zoo
zoology zoology zoology; zero zero zero; zipper zipper
```

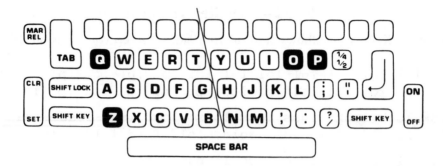

Self-Testing Work:

> apt apt apt; pot pot pot; top top top; par par par
> pool pool pool; pour pour pour; appear appear appear
>
> quite quite quite; quote quote quote; pay pay pay; paid
> quiet quiet quiet; require require require; equip equip
>
> zigzag zigzag zigzag; zero zero zero; realize realize
> ship ship ship; shop shop shop; dazzle dazzle dazzle
>
> prepare prepare prepare; prepay prepay prepay; hip hip
> play play play; pewter pewter pewter; postage postage
>
> did you sell your shop at a profit or loss last year;
> did you sell your shop at a profit or loss last year;
>
> we were happy to see you at your party last week;
> we were happy to see you at your party last week;
>
> we hope you realize that we quoted low figures to you;
> we hope you realize that we quoted low figures to you;
>
> we shall order fifty lollipops for the play group today;
> we prefer to prepay the postage for the wool suits;
>
> we ordered three gross of zippers for the good sweaters;
> you should order two quires of paper for typewriter use;
>
> for what purpose do you use the quartz that you ordered;
> they study zoology; they were all at the zoo yesterday;

Corrective Work: Practice corrections.

RELAX

Improvement Work: Type the above 20 lines again.   Aim at an accurate copy.

You have now learned 20 out of 26 letters in the alphabet.

LESSON 6

Aim: To learn
    1. To use the **shift keys** for **capital letters**
    2. To use the **colon** (:)

15 (25)

72 (82)
Single spacing

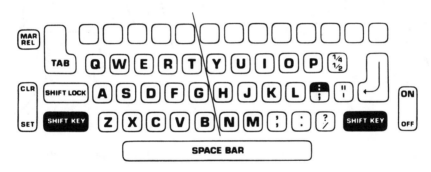

Fig. 22

Warm-up (5 minutes):

After copying and saying the drills, type the sentence ten times. The sentence contains every letter you have learned so far.

```
a'qa sws ded frf ftf fgf juj jyj jhj kik lol ;p; aza
aqa sws ded frf ftf fgf juj jyj jhj kik lol ;p; aza

keep quart water jars ready for this large freezer;
```

New Keys Shift and : (Colon)

You will find a key to the left of **Z** and another key to the right of /. These are the two shift keys. **To type** a **capital letter**, use the shift key on the opposite side of the machine. Depress the **shift key** firmly with the little finger of the opposite hand and strike the letter to be capitalized. Be sure to hold the shift key down until after the letter is struck.

Step 1—Shift Key and Colon Tryout

1. While lightly touching **S D F**, depress the **left** shift key with your **A** finger.   Return the finger to **A**.

2. While lightly touching **J K L**, depress the **right** shift key with your **semi** finger. Return the finger to **;**.

3. Practice the left and right shift key manipulation until you can perform it smoothly. (See Figs. 23 and 24.)

4. : (colon) and ; (semicolon) share the same key.   Depress the left shift key and strike the semi key to type **:**.   Feel **;**.   Feel **:**.

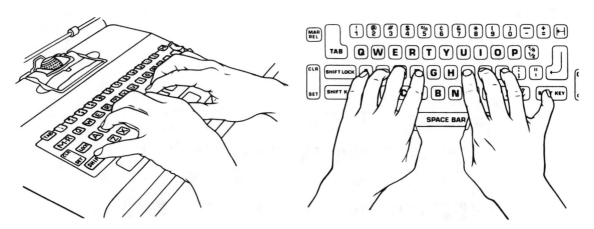

Fig. 23 Depressing the left shift key   **Fig. 24** Depressing the right shift key

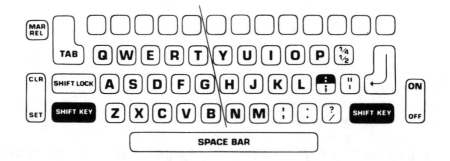

Step 2—Capital Letter and Colon Drill

1. Hold the shift key down until you have struck the letter.
2. Return the pinkie to its guide key.

> *Always space once after a semicolon.*
> *Always space twice after a colon.*

Type this line once.

; :   ; :   ; :   ; :   ; :   ; :   ; :   ; :   ; :   ; :

Learn this general rule now. When a punctuation mark has a **period** at the bottom (: ? ! .), space **twice** after it. When a punctuation mark has a **comma** at the bottom (; ,), space **once** after it.

To strike **F,** depress the **right** shift key.
To strike **J,** depress the **left** shift key.

```
F F F:  Fl Fl Fl:  Flo Flo Flo:  Flossie Flossie
J J J:  Ja Ja Ja:  Jay Jay Jay:  Jerry Jerry

Dear Sir:  Dear Sir:  Dear Sir:  Dear Sir:  Dear Sir:
```

Self-Testing Work

Test your mastery of the shift key by typing the following lines. Take your time.
REMINDER: Use the **shift key opposite** to the letter that is struck.

```
Sid Sid Sid; Ida Ida Ida; Paul Paul Paul; Zelda Zelda
Dot Dot Dot; Kay Kay Kay; Tess Tess Tess; Yale Yale Yale

Joseph likes to study; Sheila likes to study art;
Joseph likes to study; Sheila likes to study art;

The poster says:  Keep Off the Grass
The poster says:  Keep Off the Grass

Order these supplies:  two typewriters; a quart of glue
Order these supplies:  two typewriters; a quart of glue

Peter likes to play the flute for the Fellowship Group
Peter likes to play the flute for the Fellowship Group

Walter will write to Ursula Tuesday or Thursday;
Walter will write to Ursula Tuesday or Thursday;

Please order:  two dozen erasers; eight quires of paper
Please order:  two dozen erasers; eight quires of paper
```

Corrective Work: Practice corrections five times correctly.
MANUAL: If you find any capital letter raised, it is due to one of two causes: either the shift key is not held down completely or the shift key has been released too soon.

RELAX

Improvement Work: Retype the 14 lines with greater accuracy.

LESSON 7

Aim: To learn
    1. Keys **N** and **M**
    2. To use the **shift lock**

15 (25)

72 (82)
Single spacing

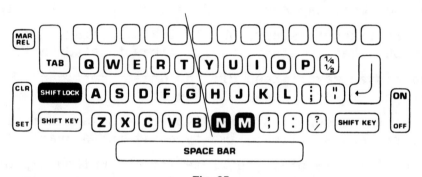

Fig. 25

Warm-up: Copy the drills. Type the sentence five times.

```
aqa sws ded frf ftf fgf juj jyj jhj kik lol ;p; aza
aqa sws ded frf ftf fgf juj jyj jhj kik lol ;p; aza
aA sS dD fF gG jJ hH kK lL ;: zZ pP oO qQ wW tT yY

Keep quart water jars ready for this large freezer;
```

New Keys N and M

Step 1—New Key Preview

The **J** finger controls both **N** and **M**. For **N**, the **J** finger should reach down and to the left on the lower line. Feel **J N J** several times.

For **M**, the **J** finger should reach down and to the right on the lower line. Feel **J M J**. Feel **J N M J**. Feel **J M N J**. Feel **J M J J N J**. Feel **M**. Feel **N**.

28

Feel all the keys that the **J** finger controls: **J U Y H N M**. Feel **J N J** and **J M J** until you know the reaches.

Step 2—New Key Tryout

```
jnj jmj jnj jmj jnj jmj jnj jmj jnj jmj jnj jmj jnj jmj
juj jyj jhj jnj jmj juj jyj jhj jnj jmj jnj jmj jnj jmj

Jane Jane Jane; June June June; junior junior junior
John John John; Jonathan Jonathan Jonathan; Joan Joan

jam jam jam; major major major; minor minor minor
man man man; James James James; Jimmy Jimmy Jimmy

maintain maintain maintain; manager manager manager
ham hem hum him; tan ten tin ton; jump hump lump;

Is this player from a major or minor league;
Are you planning to go to the game on Monday;

Sunday Monday Tuesday Wednesday Thursday Friday Saturday
Sunday Monday Tuesday Wednesday Thursday Friday Saturday
```

New Key Shift Lock

The **shift lock** is a timesaving device that enables you to type a series of capital letters. You will find the shift lock above the left shift key, just to the left of **A**.

Step 1—Shift Lock Tryout

1. With your **A** finger, reach to the left and depress the shift lock—then return the finger quickly to **A**. The machine is now locked for typing capital letters.
2. With your **A** finger, strike the left shift key; the machine is now unlocked for regular typing. (On most machines, the machine can be unlocked by striking either the left or right shift keys.)
3. Repeat the exercise of locking and unlocking the shift key several times.

Step 2—Shift Lock Drill

```
green Green GREEN; magenta Magenta MAGENTA; plum PLUM
green Green GREEN; magenta Magenta MAGENTA; plum PLUM

Do you plan to heat your house with OIL or GAS;
Do you plan to heat your house with OIL or GAS;

The manager ran this ad:  HIGH QUALITY PAPER FOR LESS
The manager ran this ad:  HIGH QUALITY PAPER FOR LESS
```

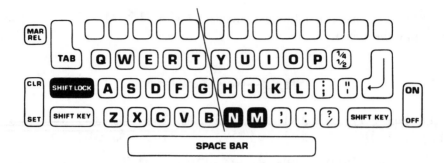

Self-Testing Work

Type these 20 lines.   Distinguish between the semicolon and colon.

REMEMBER: Leave only one space after a semicolon.

Leave two spaces after a colon.

```
may may may; name name name; mind mind mind; yam yam
nominate nominate nominate; and and and; on on on; in in

when when when; more more more; sample sample sample
payment payment payment; judgment judgment judgment

sing sing sing; ring ring ring; swing swing swing
trying trying trying; looking looking looking; jumping

The new manager is lending money to many employees
The new manager is lending money to many employees

I wish to nominate you for a national position in June
I wish to nominate you for a national position in June

The museum talk is in Spanish; do you understand it
The museum talk is in Spanish; do you understand it

Please print the following:  ALL SALES ARE FINAL
Please print the following:  ALL SALES ARE FINAL

The arrow points:  THIS WAY TO THE ZOO AND THE GARDENS
The arrow points:  THIS WAY TO THE ZOO AND THE GARDENS

Does she realize what her FINE JEWELRY is worth;
Does she realize what her FINE JEWELRY is worth;

All writers and reporters must learn to type with ease;
All writers and reporters must learn to type with ease;
```

Corrective Work: Practice corrections five times.

RELAX

Improvement Work: Retype the 20 lines with greater accuracy.

LESSON 8

Aim: To learn
1. Keys for **period** (.) and **comma** (,)
2. To use the **tabulator**

15 (25)

72 (82)
Single spacing

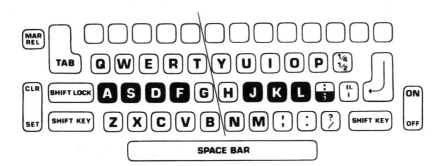

Warm-up (5 minutes): When typing the drills, say the letters to reinforce the connection between the letters and their control keys.

```
aqa sws ded frf ftf fgf juj jyj jhj kik lol ;p; aza
jnj jmj aza jnj jmj aza jnj jmj aza jnj jmj aza jnj

amaze amaze amaze; maize maize maize; numeral numeral
janitor janitor janitor; mineral mineral mineral; mine

majority majority majority; minority minority minority
quaint quaint quaint; when when when; from from from

market market market; margins margins margins; kind kind
lend lend lend; friend friend friend; drama drama drama

I was looking for a new typewriter so my friend found
this ad:  ONE DAY SALE ON TYPEWRITERS
```

31

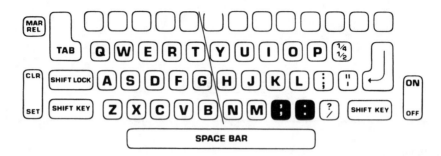

Fig. 26

New Keys . (Period) and , (Comma)

(Up to this point, the semicolon has been used in place of periods and commas. From this point on, you can use these punctuation marks correctly.)

The **L** finger controls the **period**.

The **K** finger controls the **comma**.

Step 1—New Key Preview

The Period (.)

Lightly touching **J** and **K**, move your **L** finger down and slightly to the right. Feel **L . L** until it is familiar. It is not necessary to keep your finger on the semi when reaching for the period.

The Comma (,)

Lightly touching **;** and **L**, move the **K** finger down and to the right. Your finger is now on the **comma** key. Feel **K , K** while saying the letters out loud.

Feel l . l k , k many times.

Step 2—New Key Tryout

*Space **once** after a comma.*
*Space **twice** after a period at the end of a sentence.*
*Space **once** after a period used with an abbreviation.*

```
l.l l.l l.l l.l l.l l.l l.l k,k k,k k,k k,k k,k k,k k,k
Order the following:  pens, paper, rulers, and erasers.
Order the following:  pens, paper, rulers, and erasers.

Order it now.  Order it now.  Order it now.  Order it.
Mr. Smith, Mr. Jones and Ms. Ryan attended the meeting.
```

New Key: The Tabulator

Your typewriter has a tabulator key, usually at the left above the shift lock. It may be marked TAB or bear an arrow symbol. Some typewriters have a **tabulator bar** centered above the keyboard. (See Fig. 27 and 28.) Locate the tab key on your machine. Its purpose is to make the carrier jump to any scale points you set. The tab key is used for indenting for a paragraph, tabulating information in columns, or when typing letters for jumping to preset points for the date and complimentary closing. When filling in many of the same forms, tab stops can be set for different items on the form. Near the tab key you will find keys for clearing and setting tab stops. The clearing key may be marked "Clear" or "Cl" or "T-". The setting key may be marked "Set" or "T+".

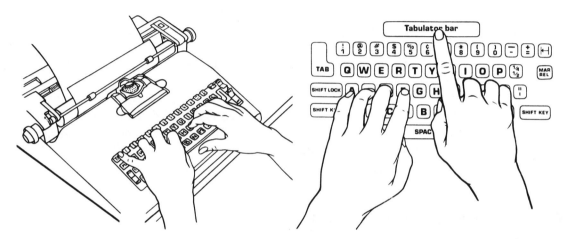

Fig. 27 Tab at left: Reach with your left pinkie.　**Fig. 28** Tab bar: Reach with your right forefinger.

Follow these steps for **indenting paragraphs:**

1. Remove tab stops already set by holding down the **clear** key as you depress the tab as many times as is needed to reach the end of the line. On many machines, tab stops can be cleared by just holding the **clear** key down as you either space across the line or RETURN.

   Test for clearing by pressing the tab key; the carrier should skip to the end of the line.

2. Set a tab stop for paragraphs (five spaces in).
   a. Tap the space bar five times.
   b. Depress the TAB SET key.
   c. RETURN and test the setting by pressing the tab key.

To use the **tab key**, hold it down with the **left pinkie** until the carrier stops. If your machine has a **tab bar**, use the **right forefinger**. *In either case, anchor your other fingers on their guide keys.*

Practice tabulating and RETURN by touch, without looking.

To clear a single tab, depress the **tab clear** at the point where it is set.

Self-Testing Work: Type each paragraph once.   When typing paragraphs with single spacing, leave an extra line space between paragraphs.   In other words, RETURN twice.

Tab set at 20 (30)

Single spacing

> Strike all keys sharply. Do not let a finger
> linger on any letter. Otherwise the impression may
> show a shadow or two letters instead of one.
>
> If you find that your fingers strike additional,
> unwanted letters, look to see if they are too
> straight. Perhaps your wrists are too low. Or perhaps
> your seat is too low. Generally, it is easier to type
> if your seat is higher rather than lower. Try any or
> all of these remedies.
>
> Your posture is important. You should sit firmly
> on your seat, not forward at the edge. Your feet should
> be flat on the floor, parallel, right foot slightly
> forward. Your arms should be at your sides. Sit up
> straight.

Corrective Work: Practice corrections five times.

RELAX

Improvement Work: Retype the three paragraphs.   Aim at accuracy.

Review of F J R U

Keyboard Review (10 minutes): The purpose of typing these eight lines is to strengthen your control of **F J R U**.   If you finish ahead of time, type them again.

KEEP YOUR EYES ON THE BOOK.

RETURN twice after every second line.

```
for fat few fur foe fit fed fee for fat fun few faze;
fan few fir fat for fee fig fin fry fit fur fat fake;

jug jig jut jar joy jag jaw jar jet jot jam jug jazz;
joy jug jog jag jaw joy jig jam jar jig jaw jog just;

rye run row red rim ray rap rug rig ran rum rug rot;
rot ram rut row red rip ray rap rug rag run rye rim:

up us use uses urge ugly until upper upmost upright;
us up urn urge uses unit under usual umpire upswing;
```

LESSON 9

Aim: 1. To learn keys **V B**
  2. To develop accuracy and increase speed through **one-minute timings**

15 (25)   72 (82)
                                                                     Single spacing

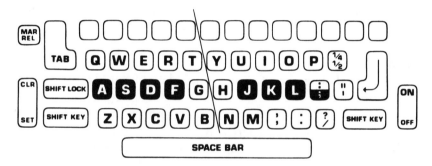

Warm-up (5 minutes): Say the letters of the drill as you type. Type the sentence as many times as you can within five minutes.

```
aqa sws ded frf ftf fgf juj jyj jhj kik lol ;p; aza jnj
jmj k,k l.l aza jnj jmj k,k l.l aza jnj jmj k,k l.l aza

You should know of some quiet, lazy, joyful trips for me.
     1     2     3     4     5     6     7     8     9    10    11
```

Practice corrections.

> NOTE: **1.** The above warm-up sentence contains eleven five-stroke words. A stroke may be a letter, a space, or a punctuation mark.
> **2.** In calculating typing speed, five strokes count as one word.

Skill-Building Work: Skill automatically comes with practice. By repeating the typing of the same sentence over and over, you will be typing it faster and more accurately.

One-Minute Timed Test

You can use an automatic timer (with a bell), or ask a friend or member of your family to time you. Use a digital watch which records seconds or an analog watch with a second hand. Type the warm-up sentence as many times as you can before the end of the minute. Then:

1. Record the number of words you typed and the number of errors you made.

2. Subtract the errors from the total words you typed to arrive at the number of correct words you typed in one minute.

> EXAMPLE: Assume that you typed 21 words and made 3 errors.
> Total words typed.................. 21
> Subtract errors...................... −3
> Correct words per minute 18

3. Practice words in which you made errors.   Always practice corrections after each timing.

4. Type two more one-minute timings.   After each timing, calculate the number of correct words per minute.

5. Compare the results of the three timings.   The highest number of words is your best score.

Progress Record

Keep a progress record of your best scores in tabulated form like the following sample:

One-Minute Timed Typing
Progress Record

Date	Lesson	Correct Words
May 1	9	18

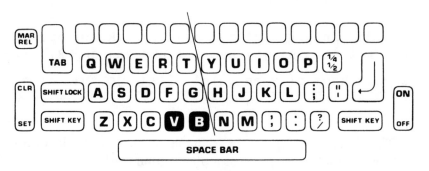

Fig. 29

New Keys V and B

The **F** finger controls both **V** and **B**.

Step 1—New Key Preview

With **F** finger, feel down and slightly to the right for **V**.   Feel **F V F** until it is familiar. Say **F V F** as you feel it.   **B** is to the right of **V**.   Feel **F V B F** several times.   Feel **F B F**.   Say and feel **F V F   F B F** until it is memorized.

Step 2—New Key Tryout

```
fvf fvf fvf fvf fvf fvbf fvbf fvbf fvbf fvbf fbf fbf fbf
fvf fbf fvf fbf fvf fbf fvf fbf fvf fbf fvf fbf fvf fbf

five five five; fever fever fever; favor favor favor;
vest vest vest; very very very; ever ever ever; every

beef beef beef; feeble feeble feeble; fable fable fable;
baffle baffle baffle; before before before before; be be

travel travel travel; brave brave brave; valuable value
big bag beg bug bog; save rave wave have pave gave grave

wives lives strives hives drives jives knives deprives
terrible trouble due to bribes; terrible trouble; bribes
```

Self-Testing Work: Type this exercise which stresses **V** and **B**.   Practice corrections.

```
verify verify verify; vague vague vague; valuable value
be been; bet better; bit bitter; bat batter; but butter

vibrate vibrate vibrate; vibes vibes vibes; tube tube
quiver quiver quiver; zebra zebra zebra; big bigger

favorite favorite favorite; fabulous fabulous fabulous
The spider wove a very fine web.  The spider wove a web.

A vast number of people like to buy big bargains.
A vast number of people like to buy big bargains.

To be, or not to be:  that is the question.
To be, or not to be:  that is the question.
```

Paragraph Practice with *double spacing*.
    Set line-space gauge at "**2.**"
    Set tab at 20 (30).
    When typing paragraphs with **double spacing**, do not leave any extra lines between paragraphs, just the regular double space.   When typing paragraphs with **single spacing**, an extra **line space** must be left between paragraphs.

    REMINDER: Space **once** after a comma and a semi.
                Space **twice** after a colon and a period.
                Indent for each paragraph with tab key.

Type the three paragraphs.

      Learning to type is like learning to drive an automobile. Typing is learned by memorizing the motions and doing them over and over. It is not done by merely having a mental image; it must be done manually.

      Learning to type is easy for anyone willing to invest some time and effort. Daily work will result in steady progress.

      Not only typists, but writers, reporters, business people, and professional people find this skill very useful. Many heads of firms like to draft their letters on a typewriter before handing them over to their typists.

Corrective Work: Practice corrections five times.

RELAX

Improvement Work: Retype the three paragraphs more smoothly and more accurately.

Review of G J T Y
Challenge Work: Test your mastery of letters **G J T Y**.

Single spacing

```
go got get gas gag gap gay gig gift gravy great;
go gin gay gem gas gab get gal give great graze;

he her has had his hit hob hut hat hay ham had have;
he his her hag him hem hum hot hub hen had has haze;

to try tip tin two tag too the try ton tap type;
to two tan tub try too the try top ten tab them;

you yes yet yam yell year yoke your yarn yore;
yap yet yes you yore yawn your yule year yell;
```

LESSON 10

Aim: 1. To complete the alphabet by learning letters **C** and **X**
2. To increase speed with one-minute timings

15 (25)

72 (82)
Single spacing

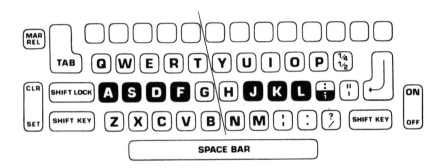

Warm-up: Say the drills as you type them.   Type the sentence five times.

```
aqa sws ded frf ftf fgf juj jyj jhj kik lol ;p; aza fvf
fbf jnj jmj k,k l.l aza fvf fbf jnj jmj k,k l.l k,k l.l
```

Many of the prizes were judged to be valuable antiques.
   1   2   3   4   5   6   7   8   9   10   11

Skill-Building Work: As in Lesson 9, test yourself with **three** one-minute timings on the above sentence.
1. Repeat the sentence as many times as you can before the end of the minute.
2. After each test:
    a. Record the number of words you typed.
    b. Subtract the number of errors from the words you typed.   An incorrect spacing, spelling, omitted word, or repeated word counts as an error.   An omitted or repeated word occurs when you look away from the book.
    c. Practice corrections after each timing.
    d. Enter the best result of the three timings on your score sheet.

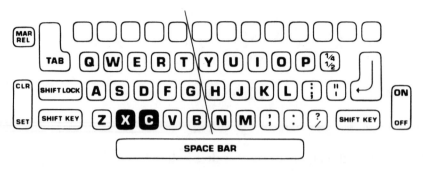

Fig. 30

New Key C

C is controlled by the **D** finger.

Step 1—New Key Preview

Lightly touching **A** and **S**, move the **D** finger down and slightly to the right to reach for **C**. (You may have to raise the **F** finger.) Feel **D C D** several times until you are comfortable with this reach. Say **D C D** as you reach.

Step 2—New Key Tryout

```
dcd dcd dcd dcd dcd dcd dcd dcd dcd dcd dcd dcd dcd dcd
cede cede cede cede cede cede cede cede cede cede cede

decide decide decide; code code code code; creed creed
decree decree decree; dice dice dice; decks decks decks

can can can; candy candy candy; cancel cancel cancel;
credit credit credit; creditor creditor creditor;

come compare company complete complaint combination
conduct contest contract contrast condense consist
```

New Key X

X is controlled by the **S** finger.

Step 1—New Key Preview

Lightly touching **A**, move the **S** finger down and slightly to the right. Feel **S X S** many times as you say it. Memorize **S X S**.

Step 2—New Key Tryout

```
sxs sxs sxs sxs sxs sxs sxs sxs sxs sxs sxs sxs sxs sxs
six six six six six six six six six six six six six six
```

sex sex sex; sextet sextet sextet; taxes taxes taxes;
wax wax wax; waxes waxes waxes; mixes mixes mixes;

boxes boxes boxes; fixes fixes fixes; textiles textiles
flexible flexible flexible; Mexico Mexico Mexico;

excel excel excel; excels excels excels; excellent
expect expect expect; exceed exceed exceed; expert
abcdefghijklmnopqrstuvwxyz abcdefghijklmnopqrstuvwxyz

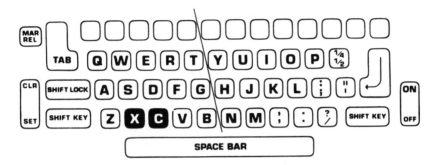

Self-Testing Work:

Space once after an abbreviation.

PART 1. Type these ten lines.

excuse excuse excuse; excused excused excused; excuses
concert concert concert; exercise exercise exercise;

lexicon lexicon lexicon; dictionary dictionary; diction
examine examine examine; track track track; crack crack

Dr. Luxemburg can come to your concert next October.
Mr. Campbell is coming home from Mexico in March.

Mr. Cox, the tax expert, will examine the tax returns.
Mr. Cox will contact you soon. Expect him in December.

You can now type every word in the dictionary except for
those words which contain a hyphen. Congratulations.

PART 2. Paragraph Practice

Double spacing
Set a tab for paragraph indentation.

REMINDER: RETURN only once between paragraphs when double spacing.

There was a fire at the box factory yesterday.

Some boxes were packed with textiles and some boxes were

packed with explosives.

Fortunately, an expert in explosives was available, and he was able to explain which chemicals would best fight the fire. There were no injuries.

Although the damage may exceed sixty thousand dollars, the houses on both sides of the box factory were untouched.

Corrective Work: Practice corrections five times.

RELAX if you need to.

Improvement Work: Retype the three paragraphs.

Review of A Q ; P (5 minutes):

```
act awe and ask; apt any art all; age able acid aged;
ace all art any; ask act add adz; axe aged able acid;

quit quip quote; quite quick queen quilt; quaint quorum
quiz quit quire; quiet quart quail queer; quest quickly

pin pup put; pull palm pant; pint peal paint; punch
pot pen pox; pour pose pear; pick push point; paper
```

LESSON 11

Aim: 1. To learn the symbols **diagonal** (/), **question mark** (?), and **hyphen** (-)
2. To develop skill in using all the letters of the alphabet

15 (25)

72 (82)
Single spacing

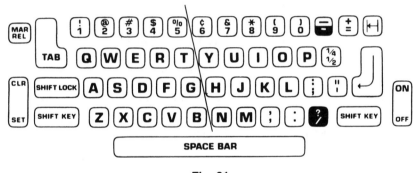

Fig. 31

Warm-up (5 minutes): After typing the drill, type the alphabetic sentence ten times.

```
aqa aza sws sxs ded dcd frf ftf fgf fbf fvf aqa aza sws
juj jyj jhj jnj jmj kik k,k lol l.l ;p; juj jyj jhj jnj

The quick brown fox jumped over the lazy dogs.
      1     2     3     4     5     6     7     8     9
```

Skill-Building Work: Test yourself on three one-minute timings on the warm-up sentence which contains all the letters in the alphabet. Follow the instructions in Lesson 10.

New Symbols / (slant or diagonal)
          ? (question mark)

The semi finger controls the key that types both / and ?.
The left shift key must be depressed to type ?.

43

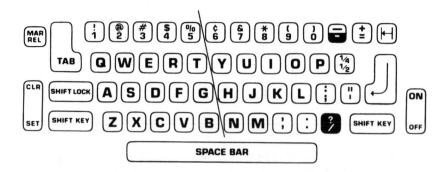

Step 1—New Key Preview / and ?

With the ; finger, feel down and to the right for /. Feel ; / ; many times, saying **semi, diagonal, semi.**

For ? (question mark) depress the left shift key. Reach with the ; finger for the / key. With the shift key down you will be typing ?. Practice feeling for / and ?.

Step 2—New Key Tryout

Space twice after ? at the end of a sentence.

```
;/; ;?; ;/; ;?; ;/; ;?; ;/; ;?; ;/; ;?; ;/; ;?; ;/; ;?;
c/o c/o c/o c/o; n/c n/c n/c n/c; c/o c/o c/o c/o c/o
Who?  When?  Where?  Why?  How?  How much?  How much?
```

New Key hyphen (–)
The semi finger also controls hyphen (–).

Step 1—New Key Preview

While touching **J K** and **L**, reach high up with the **semi** finger above **P** and slightly to the right for –. Feel ; – ; many times as you say **semi, hyphen, semi.**

Step 2—New Key Tryout

Leave *no* space either before or after a hyphen.
Strike two hyphens--**without spacing**--for a dash.

```
;-; ;-; ;-; ;-; ;-; ;-; ;-; ;-; ;-; ;-; ;-; ;-; ;-; ;-;
one-half; one-fourth; one-eighth; three-quarters;
one-half; one-fourth; one-eighth; three-quarters;

Every expert was once a beginner--with ambition.
Every expert was once a beginner--with ambition.
```

Self-Testing Work:
PART 1.

```
;-;  ;/;  ;?;  ;-;  ;/;  ;?;  ;-;  ;/;  ;?;  ;-;  ;/;  ;?;  ;-;  ;/;
The diagonal is used in the abbreviation c/o for CARE OF.

Do you know that NO CHARGE is often abbreviated to n/c?
Do you know that another name for the DIAGONAL is SLANT?

The slant is also used in writing fractions with figures.
The slant is also used in writing fractions with figures.

Can you address this letter c/o Mr. Allen today?
Can you address this letter c/o Mr. Allen today?

Buy two first-class tickets for the plane to Houston.
Buy two first-class tickets for the plane to Houston.

Are you sure that you are using an up-to-date list?
Are you sure that you are using an up-to-date list?

Old-fashioned furniture will some day be antique.
Old-fashioned furniture will some day be antique.
```

PART 2. Paragraph Practice. Copy each paragraph once.

Double spacing

Set a tab stop indented five spaces for paragraphs. In future lessons, the **indentation** itself will indicate the need for the tab stop and so it will not be mentioned.

```
     A hyphen is used both to connect and to divide.
A hyphen connects two or more words to form a compound
word.  You have already typed first-class, up-to-date,
and old-fashioned.  Some other examples are:  part-time,
left-handed, and half-hearted.

     A hyphen is used to divide a long word at the end
of a line.  The word must be divided between syllables.
You may have to consult a dictionary.

     Do you have a dictionary at your desk?  When look-
ing up words, do you find the page you need easily by
making use of the two words on the top of each page
which indicate the first and last words on the page?
```

Corrective Work: Practice corrections five times.

Improvement Work: Retype the paragraphs with greater accuracy.

Single spacing

Review of B N V M (5 minutes):

Return to guide keys quickly.
Do not look up at the end of a line.

```
bag big bug bit bud bed bid bow bale bend bank blaze
but box bed bun bid big buy bag back bale band blitz

not now nut nor note nose none next nice nine nude
now nab nag nap noun note name nail nick nest next

vim vet van vex vet vast vote very vase vice visa
vow vex via vim vat vial vine vary veto verb vain

man mix mat mug made mail main make muck much mine
mow met mix men most more many mope maze mice must
```

LESSON 12

Five-Minute Timings
Aim: To learn to type steadily for five minutes

15   (25)   72   (82)
                                                         Single spacing

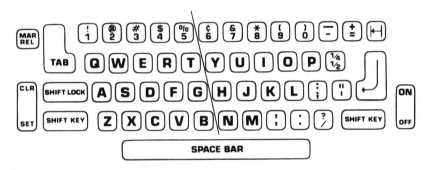

Fig. 32

Warm-up:
1. Say the drills as you type them.
2. RETURN twice and copy the first sentence five times. This sentence is the one most frequently used by typists for warm-up. Letters alternate from one hand to another.
3. RETURN twice and copy the second sentence five times. This sentence contains all the letters of the alphabet.

```
aqa aza sws sxs ded dcd frf ftf fgf fbf fvf juj jyj jhj
jnj jmj kik k,k lol l.l ;p; ;/; ;?; ;?; ;?; ;-; ;-; ;-;
```

Now is the time for all good men to come to the aid of
the party.

The quick brown fox jumped over the lazy dogs.

47

Skill-Building Work

   1. Preview Practice of Words and Phrases.   Practice each word and phrase at least three times.

```
Daily practice      touch typing     skill      easily

Once      yours      improve      cross out      Do not

errors      accuracy      practicing      fingers

correctly      which      Finish
```

                                                          Double spacing

   2. Two Five-Minute Timings

Time yourself for five minutes of steady typing on the following paragraphs, repeating the copy until the end of five minutes.

   Practice corrections after each timing.

```
                              5                        10
        Daily practice will make touch typing a skill that
                        15                      20
you can easily master.  Once mastered, this skill will
                  25
remain yours for your entire lifetime.
              30                      35
        To improve your typing while learning, do not
        40                      45
erase.  Do not cross out.  Do not strike one letter
        50                      55
over another.  Let your errors stand.  Finish every
        60
line you start.
                        65                        70
        Your accuracy is improved by correctly practicing
              75                        80
the words in which you made errors.  This trains your
              85                        90
fingers to strike the right keys.
```

   3. Calculate Your Typing Speed—after each timing.
      a. Write the total words typed in five minutes.
      b. Underline errors and subtract that number from the words typed.
      c. Divide the remainder by 5, the number of minutes you typed. The result indicates your typing speed in Correct Words per Minute.

EXAMPLE: Total words typed   101
Subtract errors   − 5
Correct words typed   5/96
Correct words per minute   19 1/5

Your typing speed in correct words is 19 words a minute. Fractions less than ½ are dropped. If the fraction is ½ or more, count it as a full word.

d. Enter the better score of the two timings on your Progress Record under a new listing as follows:

Five-Minute Timed Typing

Date	Lesson	Correct Words per Minute
June 2	12	19
3	13	20
4	14	20
5	16	21

Improvement Work: Type these paragraphs, aiming at accuracy rather than speed.

```
      There is a great variation in the speed that typ-
ing students may reach at this point.  Those who play
a musical instrument such as the piano, flute, or clar-
inet will find their fingers moving more rapidly than
those who have not exercised their fingers in this
manner.  It will take extra practice time for the latter
group to catch up, but they will.
      Those who use an electric or electronic typewriter
will find their speed higher than those who use a man-
ual typewriter.
      Just as it is easy to operate an automatic shift
car after operating a stick-shift car, it is not dif-
ficult to make the adjustment from manual to electric
or electronic.  The electric and electronic typewriters
require a lighter touch.
      Civil service examinations call for a beginning
typing speed of thirty-five words a minute.  Some
insurance companies call for forty words a minute.
Employment agencies often require fifty or fifty-five
for placement.
```

Practice corrections.

Review of X Z: The following four lines test your control of letters **X** and **Z**.   Remember that the same finger is used for **A** and **Z**, the first and last letters in the alphabet.   Type these four lines twice.

```
zip zoo zest zeal zinc zero lazy zone zoom zinc zigzag
zoo zip quiz zone lazy zinc zeal zest zero zone zenith

six vex lax tax fix extra sextet mixing taxing exhaust
fix tax vex lax six sixty expert expect except extreme
```

LESSON 13

Aim: 1. To learn key for **apostrophe** (') and **quotation** (")
2. To develop accuracy and increase speed with **th** words and timings

15 (25)

72 (82)
Single spacing

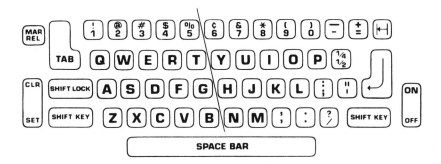

Warm-up: After typing the drills, copy each sentence five times.

```
aqa aza sws sxs ded dcd frf ftf fgf fbf fvf juj jyj jhj
jnj jmj kik k,k lol l.l ;p; ;/; ;?; ;-; ;-; ;-; ;-; ;-;
Now is the time for all good men to come to the aid of
the party.
The quick brown fox jumped over the lazy dogs.
```

Skill-Building Work: th

1. To develop speed with **th.**

Type a line of **th.** Start slowly and increase speed until you are writing **th** rapidly.
Keep control. As you type the **th** words, you will find that you can type **th** as a
unit.

```
th th th th th th th th th th th th th th th th th th
the the the these these these there there there

their their their them them them then then then
this this this think think think those those those
```

```
that that that than than than thank thank thank
math math math with with with worth worth worth

other other other either either either father father
mother mother mother brother brother brother another
```

2. Preview Practice on words and phrases
Practice each word and phrase at least three times.

```
struck      even       metronome      common      combinations
consist     succeeding      lessons        practice      unit
of these    suffixes      frequently     can be      rapidly
```

3. Two One-Minute Timings

Double spacing

```
                               5                          10
     As you develop speed in typing, you will find that
                     15                       20
keys are not struck with the even timing of a metro-
                   25                       30
nome.  Some common combinations of letters are typed
            34
together faster.
```

Practice corrections after each timing.   Enter the better of your two scores on your Progress Record under One-Minute Timings.

Stand up, stretch, breathe deeply, and shake your hands.   When you resume typing, check your typing position: sit well back on your seat; your spine should be straight, shoulders down, feet flat on the floor with one foot forward; your fingers should be naturally curved on the guide keys.

4. Two Five-Minute Timings
If you should finish before the five minutes are up, start again.

```
                             5                            10
     As you develop speed in typing, you will find that
                   15                       20
keys are not struck with the even timing of a metro-
                   25                       30
nome.  Some common combinations of letters are typed
```

```
                    35                              40
together faster.  These combinations may consist of
                45
two, three or even four letters.
            50                          55
    In succeeding lessons you will practice many of
        60                          65
these letter combinations.  Some are suffixes.  Others
    70                          75                      80
are groups of letters that appear frequently and can be
                            85                      90  91
typed rapidly as a unit.  You have already practiced th.
```

Practice corrections after each timing.

Calculate your speed according to the example in Lesson 12. Enter your better score under Five-Minute Timings.

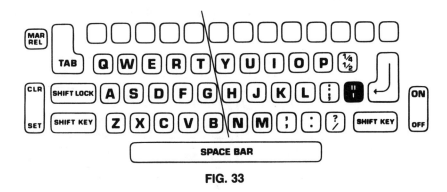

FIG. 33

Single spacing

New Symbols ' (apostrophe) and " (quotation mark)

The **semi** finger controls the key that types ' and ". The **quotation mark** requires the use of the left shift key. (See MANUAL.)

Step 1—New Key Preview ' "

With the **semi** finger, reach to the right. Keep **J K L** fingers on those keys. Feel **; ' ;** until you are comfortable with the reach.

Now depress the left shift key and reach to the same key at the right for ". Feel **; ' ;   ; " ;.**

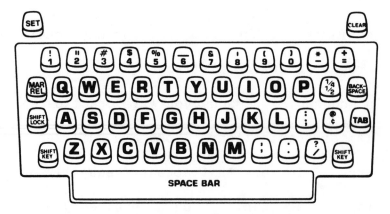

Fig. 34 The Manual Typewriter Keyboard

On the MANUAL typewriter the apostrophe (') is on the **8** key. Reach with the **K** finger for **k i 8 k**. Depress the left shift key when you reach for **8** and you will type **k i ' k**. Feel for **k ' k**. (Hold on to ; and **L** as you reach.)

The quotation mark (") is on the **2** key. Reach with the **S** finger for **s w 2 s**. Depress the right shift key when you reach for **2** and you will type **sw"s**. Feel for **s " s**. (Hold on to **D** and **F** as you reach.)

When drills for ' and " are given for electric and electronic machines, substitute **k'k** and **s"s** for MANUAL.

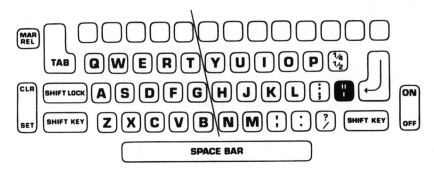

Step 2—New Key Tryout

```
;';  ;';  ;';  ;';  ;';  ;';  ;';  ;";  ;";  ;";  ;";  ;'";  ;'";
don't don't don't doesn't doesn't doesn't I'll I'll

Mary's Mary's Mary's Richard's Richard's Richard's
James' James' James' Moses' Moses' Moses' boy's boys'

There are four s's and four i's in Mississippi.
Amy read "Gone With the Wind" last summer.

George Washington is called "The Father of Our Country."
"We'll meet at the theater," said the actress.

The Royal Shakespeare Company's production of "Macbeth"
will move from London to Broadway next week.
```

Self-Testing Work: Paragraph Practice.

Double spacing

```
    Let us note the many uses of an apostrophe in the
preceding sentences as well as other uses.
    An apostrophe is used to indicate the omission of
one or more letters as in "I'll."
    An apostrophe indicates possession as in "Mary's."
    Use an apostrophe for the plural of a number or a
letter as in "four i's" or in "six 5's."  Also use it
for the plural of a name as in "three Smith's on the
payroll."
    Following a numeral, an apostrophe is an abbrevia-
tion for feet; a ditto mark, like a quotation mark, is an
abbreviation for inches.
```

Corrective Work: Practice corrections.

Challenge Work: Try to type these two paragraphs perfectly as you pay attention to the rules.

Double spacing

```
    An apostrophe is spaced as if it were a letter in
a word.  There is no space before or after an apostrophe
if it is in the middle of a word.  When an apostrophe
ends a word, space once after the apostrophe as you
would for a letter.
    These are the rules for spacing when quotation
marks are used.  Leave no space between the quotation
marks and the words they enclose.  At the close of a
quotation, a quotation mark is typed after a period or
comma.  A quotation mark is typed before a semicolon
or colon.
```

LESSON 14

Aim: To learn
      To use the **backspace key**
      Horizontal centering
      To pivot
      To build speed with **ing**
      To develop sustained typing with five-minute timings

15 (25)   72 (82)

Single Spacing

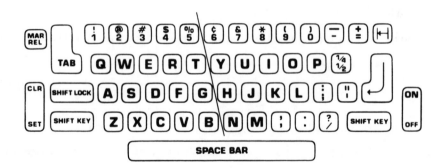

Warm-up: Say the letters as you type the drill. Type each sentence five times.

```
aqa aza sws sxs ded dcd frf ftf fgf fbf fvf juj jyj jhj
jnj jmj kik k,k lol l.l ;p; ;/; ;?; ;'; ;"; ;-; ;-; ;-;
```

Now is the time for all good men to come to the aid of
the party.

The quick brown fox jumped over the lazy dogs.

Skill-Building Work: ing

1. Type a line of **ing**, starting slowly and increasing speed.   When typing the rest of the exercise, type **ing** as a unit.

```
ing ing ing ing ing ing ing ing ing ing ing ing ing ing
sing sing sing ring ring ring wing wing wing swing swing

string string cling cling bring bring zing zing fling
singing singing ringing ringing swinging swinging

adding doing going having trying walking running
typing eating drinking sitting working playing reading

dancing quoting rising making jumping hiking skiing
moving laughing crying exciting selling going loving

Robert is realizing how much training is needed before
qualifying for a swimming and life-saving certificate.
```

2. **Preview Practice for timed copy—three times each.**

```
backspace      time-saving     devices      centering
pivoting       chosen       indicator     punctuation
of the        so that the     at the
```

3. **Two One-Minute Timings:**

Double spacing

```
                        5                        10
The backspace key is one of the most useful time-
              15                        20
saving devices on your typewriter.  You use it to back-
          25                    30        32
space if you have accidentally touched the space bar.
```

REMINDER: Practice errors after each timing.   Record the better timing.

4. Two Five-Minute Timings

```
                                5                              10
        The backspace key is one of the most useful time-
                        15                          20
saving devices on your typewriter.  You use it to back-
                        25                          30
space if you have accidentally touched the space bar.
                    35                          40
You use it for centering headings and for pivoting.
                    45                              50
        To pivot means to type a line so that the last
                    55                          60
letter is at the right margin or other chosen point.
                65                          70
For example, if you want a date line to end at the right
    75                          80                          85
margin, bring your printing point indicator to the right
                        90                          95
margin and backspace once for each stroke--letters,
                        100                         105
punctuation marks, spaces--in the date line.  Then type
                110                         115             120
the date.  The date will then end at the right margin.
```

NOTE: Enter the better result on your Progress Record. Is your score improving?
A little improvement every day adds up to a great improvement. You may sometimes
remain on a plateau for a while. Find out which keys slow you down and practice
words with those letters. You may want to go back to the lesson that introduced
those letters. You will soon see progress.

New Work: The Backspacer

New Key Preview

Depending on your machine, the backspace key will be found at the extreme upper
right or upper left of your keyboard. It will be marked BACK or with an arrow pointing
to the left.

1. While anchoring three fingers on the guide keys, reach with your pinkie for the
backspacer. Reach for the backspacer several times, returning the pinkie to the
guide key.
2. Depress the backspacer. Your printing element will move one space to the left.
Your machine may have a repeat backspacer; in that case, if you keep the backspacer
depressed, it will continue to backspace.

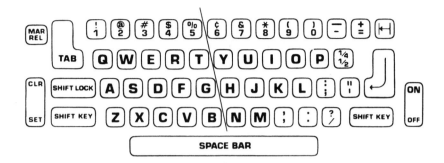

Single spacing

New Work: Pivoting

To pivot we will start at the right margin, 72 or 82, and backspace for every stroke in the line. Thus each line will end at the right margin.

New Work Tryout

To pivot for

NEW SCHOOL FOR SOCIAL RESEARCH
Office of the President

1. Bring carrier to the right-hand margin.
2. Backspace for each stroke as you say: N E W space S C H O O L space F O R space S O C I A L space R E S E A R C H
3. Type the line: NEW SCHOOL FOR SOCIAL RESEARCH
4. Pivot for the line: Office of the President
5. Type the line: Office of the President

Double spacing

Self-Testing Work: Pivot and type the following:

EATON's Corrasable Typewriter Paper
CORRASABLE BOND
MATCHING ENVELOPES

New Work: Horizontal Centering

Horizontal centering means typing a word or a line across the paper so that the left and right margins are equal.

To center horizontally:
1. Clear tab stops and set a tab stop at the center of the paper—42 for pica; 50 for elite.
2. From the center of the paper, backspace **once** for each **two** strokes in the material to be centered. If one letter is left over, ignore it.

New Work Tryout

1. To center the word GENEROSITY
   a. Tab key to center (42 or 50).
   b. Backspace once for each two strokes as you say: GE NE RO SI TY
   c. With the shift key locked, type the word.
2. To center the word EDUCATION
   a. Tab key to center.
   b. Backspace once for each two strokes as you say: ED UC AT IO (disregard N).
   c. Type the word.
3. To center the name FRANKLIN D. ROOSEVELT
   a. Tab key to center.
   b. Backspace once for each two strokes as you say: FR AN KL IN space D period space RO OS EV EL (disregard T).
   c. Type the name.

If you have an electronic typewriter with **automatic centering**, follow the instructions in the manual.

Self-Testing Work: Center each of the following lines in *double spacing*. RETURN twice after each group.

MADE SIMPLE BOOKS

A DOUBLEDAY PUBLICATION

THE BRIDGE OF SAN LUIS REY

by

Thornton Wilder

NEW YORK UNIVERSITY

School of Law

Annual Homecoming

THE ROYAL OPERA HOUSE, COVENT GARDEN

presents

Joan Sutherland and Luciano Pavarotti

in LUCIA DI LAMMERMOOR

SOPHISTICATED LADY

JEANETTE KIMBALL

Trios and Quartets

"BITS and BYTES"

on

Channel Thirteen

THE COMPUTER

SHOW

THAT EVEN ADULTS

CAN

UNDERSTAND

LESSON 15

Aim: To learn to use the **margin release**
To learn how to divide words at the end of a line
To build speed with **tion**
To develop sustained typing skill by five-minute timings

15 (25)   72 (82)

Single spacing

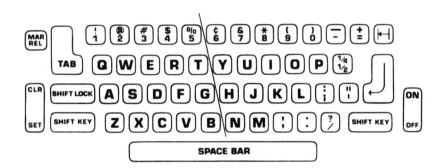

Warm-up: Type the drills as you say the letters.
Type the alphabetic sentence ten times.

```
aqaza swsxs dedcd frftfgfbfvf jujyjhjnjmj kik,k lol.l
;p;/; ;?; ;'; ;"; ;-; ;/; ;?; ;'; ;"; ;-; ;-; ;-; ;-;
```

```
Zelda quickly mixed the very big jar of new soap flakes.
```

Skill-Building Work: tion

1. Type a line of **tion**, starting slowly and gradually increasing speed. In the words following, type **tion** as a unit.

```
tion tion tion tion tion tion tion tion tion tion tion
nation nation nation notion notion notion station station
```

```
ration lotion direction situation application motion
promotion tuition sensation destination computation
```

61

compensation consideration dissertion punctuation
celebration liberation restoration creation recreation

narration elevation affection affectation election
reaction relaxation reduction realization quotation

inflation completion junction location evaluation
compilation dispensation oration erudition elation

    For many people, a vacation means relaxation, rec-
reation and restoration of good health. For others, a
vacation means action: a liberation from routine
through travel, a celebration of new visual and mental
sensations.

2. Preview Practice—three times each

bell   warn   approaching   six   across
number   spaces   listen   automatically
margin release

Double spacing

REMINDER: Set two tabs—one for paragraphs and one for centering. It saves time
to keep a tab stop set at the center.

3. Two One-Minute Timings

5

    The bell on your typewriter rings to warn you that
15   20
you are approaching the end of a line. On some machines
25   30
the bell will ring five spaces before the end of the
33
line.

After the recording of your better score, center the heading

THE BELL

4. Two Five-Minute Timings

```
                    5                                    10
        The bell on your typewriter rings to warn you that
                    15                              20
    you are approaching the end of a line.  On some machines
                    25                          30
    the bell will ring five spaces before the end of the
                    35                          40
    line.  On other machines the bell will ring six, seven
                45                          50
    or eight spaces before the end of the line.
                        55                          60
        When you finish this timing, space across your
                    65                          70
    paper, listen for the bell, and count the number of
                    75                          80
    spaces beyond the bell to the margin stop.  Keep this
                85
    number in mind.
                            90                              95
        If the bell rings when you are in the middle of a
                        100                         105
    word, finish the word and return for a new line without
                    110                             115
    taking your eyes off the copy.  If the bell rings at
                120                             125
    the end of a word, you can type a short word, up to the
            130                         135                     140
    number of spaces before the margin.  If you are stopped
                        145                         150
    by your margin with an extra letter or two to finish the
                    155                         160
    word, use your margin release about which you will
                    165
    learn in this lesson.
                            170                             175
        You will soon respond to the bell automatically.
                        180                     184
    Return for a new line without looking up.
```

The above exercise is longer than you can type at this time in five minutes. After you practice corrections, read the exercise for content.

Margin Release

Your machine has a key, the **margin release,** that will permit you to type beyond the margin on the right or type in front of the margin at the left. It is primarily used to complete a word at the end of a line.

Check your machine. The margin-release key is either at the extreme upper left or upper right of the keyboard in the opposite position to the backspacer. It may be marked M-R or it might have a double arrow symbol.

 Fig. 35 Some margin release keys bear a double arrow symbol.

New Key Preview

a. Touching the three guide keys, reach with the appropriate pinkie to the **margin release,** depressing and immediately releasing it. Repeat several times.
b. Space to the end of the line. Depress the margin release and release it.
c. You will find that you can space and type beyond the margin.

If you type up to three letters beyond the margin to finish a word, you can still have a fairly even margin. Beyond three letters, the word should be divided if possible. Besides consulting a dictionary for proper syllabication, you can follow some general rules.

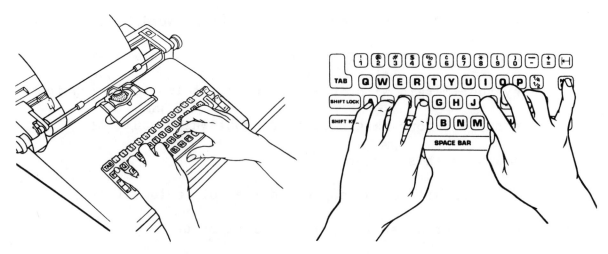

Fig. 36 Margin release at left

Fig. 37 Margin release at right

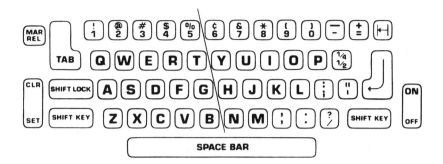

Challenge Work: RETURN twice between rules. Absorb the meaning as you type. Use the margin release when necessary. Center the heading.

RULES FOR DIVIDING WORDS AT THE END OF A LINE

Divide a word only between syllables—a syllable has a vowel sound. EXAMPLES: con-tain, pro-gram, trans-act.

Do not divide words of one syllable. EXAMPLES: thought, planned, eighth, please.

Divide a word between double consonants. EXAMPLES: col-lect, com-ment, neces-sary.

Divide a word before a suffix of three or more letters. EXAMPLES: arriv-ing, state-ment, desir-able, revers-ible, vol-uble, independ-ence, posi-tion.

When the final letter of a word is doubled before adding -ing, divide the word between the doubled consonants. EXAMPLES: sit-ting, plan-ning, begin-ning, stop-ping.

However, if a word ends in a double consonant, keep the original word intact. EXAMPLES: add-ing, tall-est, fulfill-ing.

Divide a word after a prefix. EXAMPLES: com-pany, sub-mit, dis-appoint.

Divide a hyphenated word only at the hyphen. EXAMPLES: self-confidence, attorney-at-law, cross-reference.

Do not divide proper names. EXAMPLES: Samuel, Saturday, Philadelphia.

Do not separate the title, degree or initial from the name. EXAMPLES: G. B. Shaw, Mr. Alexander, Ms. E. Allen, Dr. Miller, James Gold, Ph.D.

Do not divide contractions or abbrevations: EXAMPLES: FBI, c.o.d., wasn't.

Do not divide words of five letters or less. EXAMPLES: only, upon, carry, heavy.

Do not leave a single letter at the end of a line or carry over less than three letters. EXAMPLES: ahead, tested, rather, lovely.

Do not separate a month from the day in a date. EX-AMPLES: July 4, October 12, February 22.

Do not divide the last word of a paragraph or a page. Do not overdo the division of words.

WHEN IN DOUBT ABOUT CORRECT SYLLABICATION, CONSULT A DICTIONARY.

Corrective Work: Type corrections five times. Refer to this page from time to time, particularly when you type letters.

LESSON 16

Aim: To learn how to type from print
To build speed with **ment**
To increase skill with five-minute timings

15 (25)

72 (82)

Single spacing

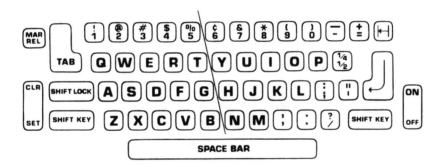

Warm-up: Type the first three lines. Type each sentence five times.

```
;/; ;?; ;/; ;?; ;'; ;"; ;'; ;"; ;-; ;-; ;-; ;-; ;-; ;-;
        Shall I send the letter "first-class, registered"
c/o Evans' Clothing Company in Buffalo, New York?

Now is the time for all good men to come to the aid of
the party.

The quick brown fox jumped over the lazy dogs.
```

Skill-Building Work: ment

1. Type a line of **ment,** starting slowly and increasing speed. If you lose control, slow down. In subsequent words, type **ment** as a unit.

```
ment ment ment ment ment ment ment ment ment ment ment
payment payment payment; statement statement statement

compliment complement settlement treatment shipment
equipment requirement adjustment supplement investment
```

67

judgment development experiment endorsement argument
installment consignment sentiment announcement raiment

apartment establishment inducement development comment
assignment instrument achievement acknowledgment

amendment temperament predicament management indictment
fulfillment environment excitement government element
assessment arraignment allotment embarrassment ailment

The company requests payment in settlement of bills
within ten days after receipt of its statement.

The government's commitment to the improvement of the
environment was an inducement for the management to give
its aid and endorsement toward the development and fulfillment of the plan to beautify our avenues.

NOTE: Many of the **ment** words are among those that are frequently misspelled.
Test yourself by typing them while someone dictates them to you. Although the
words **judgment** and **acknowledgment** are the preferred forms, **judgement** and
acknowledgement are acceptable. For **installment, instalment** is also acceptable.

2. Preview Practice—each word and phrase three times.

preceding   exercises   copying   length   printed
"justified"   extra   according   successive
previous   necessary   spaces   absolute   in the
at the   to the   and the   with the   of the

Double spacing

3. Two One-Minute Timings

                         5   10
     In preceding exercises you have been copying from
                    15   20
typed copy with the margins and the length of lines the
               25   27
same as on your typing paper.

Practice corrections and enter score.

Center the heading

TYPING FROM PRINTED COPY

4. Two Five-Minute Timings

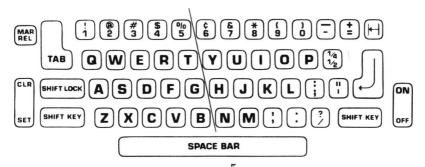

In preceding exercises you have been copying from
typed copy with the margins and the length of lines the
same as on your typing paper.

However, you may have to type from printed copy
where the length of the line will be different from a
typed copy. Printed copy may have smaller or larger
type. Printed copy usually has an even right margin--
we call this "justified."

Since you will have to determine when to start a
new line, you must listen for the bell, finish a word
or even type an extra short word, and, if necessary,
divide a word according to the rules in the previous
lesson. Try to avoid dividing words on three successive
lines.

Here is an old rule: "For an even right margin,
try not to stop more than three spaces before the margin
nor type more than three spaces beyond the margin."
But this is not absolute.

Practice corrections. Enter score.

New Work: Typing from Printed Copy
Review
a. The rules for division of words in Lesson 15.
b. The information in the five-minute timed copy you just completed.

Self-Testing Work
Type the following exercises in *double spacing*. In each case
a. Center the **heading,** using the tab which is set at the middle of the line and backspacing once for two strokes.
b. RETURN twice. (You write on the fourth line with three lines blank.)
c. Using your usual margins, indent for paragraphs.
d. Type an attractive copy.

Exercise A.

Twentieth-Century Technology

As a result of twentieth-century technology, greater changes in life style have occurred in this century than in any of the previous centuries. Our great-grandparents living in the nineteenth century did not have the convenience of electricity, automobiles, telephones, radios, refrigerators, washers, dryers, dishwashers, frozen foods, food processors, word processors, television, computers, airplanes—just to mention a few things we take for granted. There is no question that life is easier, that we have more time for recreational activities, that we can see more of the world. The question remains, "Are we happier?"

Exercise B.

PREAMBLE
of the
CONSTITUTION OF THE UNITED STATES—1787

WE THE PEOPLE of the United States, in Order to form a more perfect Union, establish Justice, insure domestic Tranquility, provide for the common defence, promote the general Welfare, and secure the Blessings of Liberty to ourselves and our Posterity, do ordain and establish this CONSTITUTION for the United States of America.

20   (30)   67   (75)

Exercises C and D.

Copy from printed matter. (a) Choose an editorial from a newspaper and type it with an acceptable right margin. (b) Choose a short magazine article or a page from a book and copy it.

LESSON 17

Aim: To learn **vertical centering** (equal top and bottom margins)
To build speed with **ly**
To develop sustained typing skill with five-minute timings

15   (25)

72   (82)
Single spacing

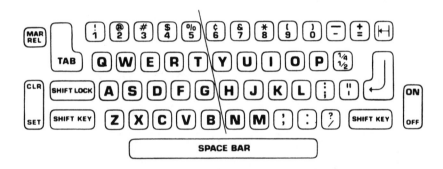

Warm-up: Type the first 2 lines.   Type the alphabetic sentence ten times.

```
abcdefghijklmnopqrstuvwxyz abcdefghijklmnopqrstuvwxyz
k,k l.l ;/; ;?; ;'; ;"; ;-; k,k l.l ;/; ;?; ;'; ;"; ;-;

Zelda quickly mixed the very big jar of new soap flakes.
```

Skill-Building Work: ly

1. Type a line of **ly**, starting slowly and increasing speed.
In the words following, type **ly** as a unit.

```
ly ly ly ly ly ly ly ly ly ly ly ly ly ly ly ly ly ly
sly sly sly; fly fly fly; ply ply ply; July July July;

daily fairly truly rarely early lately recently barely
queerly quickly quietly finally merely merrily warily

greedily steadily narrowly placidly excitedly partly
completely comfortably vertically horizontally justly

Sally weekly monthly yearly slowly hastily promptly
family accidentally efficiently readily carelessly
```

71

Daily practice will truly result in completely mastering typewriting. It can be easily and comfortably done.

An airline advertisement about fairly cheap rates for flying to Florida in July made Sally decide to fly.

An advertisement should be centered vertically and horizontally on the paper. It should be attractive.

2. Preview Practice—each word or phrase three times.

equal	bottom	number	eleven	vertical
inch	Subtract	centering	sixty-six	
available	remainder	edge	Ignore	fraction
on the	you can	so that	from the	

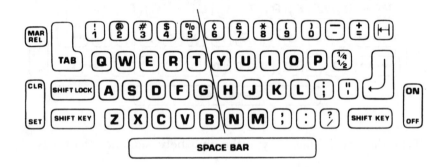

Double spacing

3. Two One-Minute Timings

```
                          5                              10
    You have learned how to center horizontally so that
                     15                        20
    the left and right margins are even.  In this lesson you
                  25                        30
    will learn how to center vertically so that the top and
              35        37
    bottom margins are even.
```

REMINDER: Practice corrections after each timing so that the errors will not be repeated.

Center the heading

VERTICAL CENTERING

4. Two Five-Minute Timings

```
                                    5                        10
         You have learned how to center horizontally so that
                         15                      20
     the left and right margins are even.  In this lesson you
                     25                      30
     will learn how to center vertically so that the top and
                 35
     bottom margins are even.
                     40                          45
         The standard typing paper is eleven inches long.
             50                          55
     Measure your paper.  All typewriters are geared to six
         60                      65
     line spaces to the vertical inch.  Thus you can type
         70                      75
     sixty-six lines on a standard sheet of paper.
                 80                      85
         To center material vertically, count the number of
         90                      95                      100
     lines in the material--typed lines and blank lines be-
                 105                         110
     tween.  Subtract this number from sixty-six, the total
             115                         120
     number of lines on the paper.  Divide the remainder by
         125                         130
     two to determine the number of lines from the top edge
     135                 140                 144
     on which to start typing.  Ignore a fraction.
```

When you enter your score on the chart, you may find that you did not improve today. If that is so, it is due to the fact that this material may be more difficult to type. All material is not of equal difficulty.

New Work: Vertical centering (top and bottom margins equal)

Refer to the last paragraph of the timed copy VERTICAL CENTERING as you do this arithmetic.

To center an ad of 26 lines vertically:

  66 lines on page

 − 26 lines in material to be centered (typed and blank)

 2/$\overline{40}$ lines remaining for both top and bottom margins

  20 lines down from top edge.

Use this as a model.

New Work Tryout: Center the following advertisement, vertically and horizontally. (The numbers on the right indicate the lines used in the ad.)

For Sale	1
(2 double)	
SALMON FISHING CAMP	5
ON THE	7
RESTIGOUCHE RIVER	9
Quebec	11
(2 double)	
For a Prospectus	15
Write to	17
Jones & Warren	19
Hotel Diplomat, Quebec	21

Follow these steps:

 a. Clear all tab stops except the one at the center—42 (50).

 b. Since this ad is in *double spacing*, check line space gauge.

 c. Count all the lines in the ad. (They are counted for you at the right.) This ad uses 21 lines.

 d. 66 − 21 = 45.

 e. 45 ÷ 2 = 22½. Ignore the fraction.

 f. Line space 22 lines from the top edge. (11 double spaces)

 g. Center the first line For Sale

 h. RETURN twice (two double spaces) and center the second line **SALMON FISHING CAMP**

 i. Double space and center the next three lines.

 j. RETURN twice and center For a Prospectus

 k. RETURN (one double space) for each of the next three lines to be centered.

Is the ad attractively placed on the paper?

Self-Testing Work: Center each of the next two ads vertically and horizontally.   By observation, you can judge the spacing: single, double, triple, or two doubles. Or you may wish to make a scale at the left edge of a card or paper for accurate measuring:

```
1
2
3
4
5
6, etc.
```

```
(1)  FOR IMMEDIATE OCCUPANCY
     HEADQUARTERS LOCATION


     You Are Cordially Invited
     To Lease Luxury Office Space At


     NORTH HILLS TOWER
     Community Road, North Hills, North Carolina


     A MAGNIFICENT NEW OFFICE BUILDING
```

Single spacing

```
(2)  DISCOVER

     The EXCITEMENT of Computers
     and
     The FUN of Camping

     at

     Holly Lodge, Arverne Road
     Ashton, Connecticut

     One and Two Week Sessions for Teenagers
```

Center Exercises 3 and 4, each on a half sheet. A half sheet has 33 lines. Subtract the lines used from 33. Divide by 2. Line space down from the top edge.

(3) Come to SHERATON
Come to LUXURY

SHERATON
Hotels, Inns & Resorts Worldwide

Call Us
Or
Call Your Travel Agent

(4) DOWN COMFORTERS
and
DOWN PILLOWS

Save Half the Retail Price

FACTORY DIRECT PRICES

The Down Store
Richmond Hill, Nebraska

Challenge Work: Center this advertisement attractively on a full sheet. Decide on your own line spacing.

ADULT EDUCATION

THE NEW SCHOOL

Sixty-six West Twelfth Street

New York City

DAY, EVENING, AND WEEKEND CLASSES

More Than a Thousand Courses

REGISTER NOW

for the

SPRING TERM

LESSON 18

Aim: To learn
     Numbers: **4** and **7**
     Symbols: **$ (dollar sign)** and **& (ampersand)**
  To build speed with: **ough**
  Five-minute timings

15 (25)

72 (82)

Single spacing

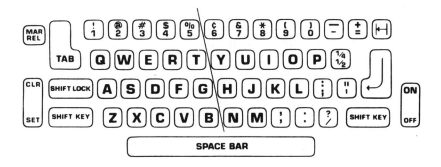

Warm-up: After the drill, type the alphabetic sentence ten times.

```
aqaza swsxs dedcd frftfgfbfvf jujyjhjnjmj kik,k lol.l
;p;/; ;:; ;-; ;'; ;"; ;?; ;:; ;-; ;'; ;"; ;?; ;:; ;-;
```

```
Pack my box with five dozen jugs of liquid veneer.
```

Skill-Building Work: ough

1. Type a line of **ough,** starting slowly and increasing speed. Copy the rest of the exercise, typing **ough** as a unit.

```
ough ough ough ough ough ough ough ough ough ough ough
though though though though though though though though

ought thought through rough tough bough bought brought
enough sought nought wrought cough fought thorough

drought Poughkeepsie dough doughty doughnut roughly
thoroughly thoughtfully thoughtlessly plough trough
```

Have we bought enough metal for the wrought iron fence?
We ought to avoid walking through this tough area.

Liza thought that her cough was brought on by rough
weather; a drought was followed by thoroughly cold days.

2. Preview Practice—three times each.

```
Except      symbols      editorial      article
newspaper      magazine      lyrics      attractively
neglect      newspaper      tabulations      business
corrections      you can      you have      you must
Of course      do not
```

Double spacing

3. Two One-Minute Timings

```
                               5                        10
        Except for numbers and symbols, you can now type
                          15                    20
an editorial or article from a newspaper or magazine.
                     25                    30
You can type a report.  You can type the lyrics to a
   32
song.
```

4. Two Five-Minute Timings If you should finish before the five minutes are up,
start at the beginning again.

```
                               5                        10
        Except for numbers and symbols, you can now type
                          15                    20
an editorial or article from a newspaper or magazine.
                     25                    30
You can type a report.  You can type the lyrics to a
                35                    40
song.  You can type a notice or an advertisement and
           45
center it attractively.
                          50                    55
        Since you have come this far, do not neglect your
           60                    65
daily work with this book.  Besides learning to type
```

70   75

```
       70                              75
numbers and symbols, which are essential, you must learn
   80                      85                          90
how to set up letters and tabulations, type envelopes,
                          95                  100
and fill in business forms.  In lessons following, you
                105                      110
will learn how to type on lines.  You will learn how
              115                      120
to make changes and corrections on a page of typing.
            125                  130
        Of course, you must continue to type with greater
          135                  139
accuracy and build up speed.
```

REMINDER: Practice corrections after each timing.   Enter scores.

TYPING TIP: If you are making more than five errors in a five-minute timing, slow down a bit.   Type with better control of your fingers.   Speed will naturally follow regular practice.

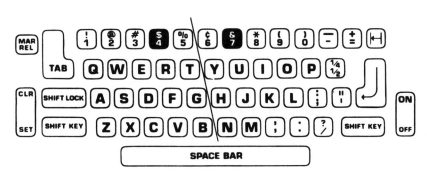

Fig. 38

Single spacing

New Keys   4 $ (Dollar Sign) and 7 & (Ampersand)

   1. 4 and $ use the same key, controlled by the **F** finger.   Depress the right shift key for $.

Step 1—New Key Preview 4 $

While keeping **A S D** fingers on the guide keys, reach with the **F** finger to **R** and in the same direction above **R** to **4**.   Feel **f r 4 r f**.   Feel **f r 4 f**.   Feel **f 4 f** several times.

Depress the right shift key and feel for **4**.   You are now reaching for $.

Without the shift key, reach for **4**.   With the shift key, reach for $.   Memorize **f 4 f f $ f**.

Step 2—New Key Tryout

```
fr4rf fr4rf fr4rf fr4f fr4f fr4f f4f f4f f4f f$f f$f f$f
$4 $4 $4 $4 $4 $4 $4 $44 $44 $44 $444 $444 $444 $44.44
```

```
On Sale:  Cassettes, $4.44; Illustrated Books, $44.44;
Fine Cloth Coats, $444.44; Luxury Fur Coats, $4,444.44
```

NOTE: There are no spaces within the figures.

2. **7** and **&** use the same key, controlled by the **J** finger.   Depress the left shift key for **&**.

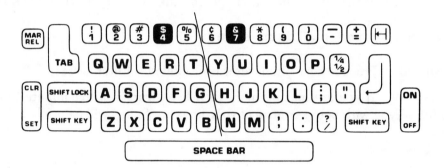

Step 1—New Key Preview 7 &

While keeping **;** **L K** fingers on the guide keys, reach with the **J** finger to **U** and above **U** in the same direction to **7**.   Feel **j u 7 u j**.   Feel **j u 7 j**.   Feel **j 7 j** several times.

Depress the left shift key and feel for **7**.   You are now reaching for **&**.
Without the shift key, reach for **7**.   With the shift key, reach for **&**.

NOTE: Leave a space after the ampersand.

Space once after an initial or abbreviation.

Step 2—New Key Tryout

```
ju7uj ju7uj ju7uj ju7j ju7j j7j j7j j7j j&j j&j j&j j&j
77 777 74 747 7,777 7,477 $7 $77 $77.44 $744,744 $4,747
```

```
Carter & Co., Lord & Taylor, Blake & Sons, E. & J. Fox.
B. Altman & Co. is selling bath towels for $7.47.
```

Self-Testing Work: Part 1. *Single spacing*

```
f4f f4f f4$f f4$f f$f f$f f4f f$f f4f f$f f4f f$f f4f
j7j j7j j7&j j7&j j&j j&j j7j j&j j7j j&j j7j j&j j7j
```

Tickets $4 and $7; Tickets $4 and $7; Tickets on sale at R. H. Macy & Co., Doubleday & Company, Abraham & Straus.

47th Street Exchange is offering dry copiers for $747.74. James & Ellis are moving on May 7 from 74th St. to 47th.

Fly on a 747 on July 4 for $744, round-trip to Europe. Meet me at 7:47 p.m. at the airport on April 7.

Part 2. *Double spacing.*

Crane & Co. are going out of business on June 4. To clear out their entire stock, they offer fine wool suits, formerly sold at $447, at the bargain price of $77.47. Come early for a full selection.

Mail a statement to each of the following firms showing the amount due: Jones & Aaron, $474.44; Fairbanks & Ryan, $74.77; Tremont & Company, $4,444.77; Hopkins & Sons, $747.44.

Fabre & Brothers, fashion designers, are selling their Sample Coats, usually $777, at the end-of-season price of $474. They also offer Designer Suits, formerly $474, at the end-of-season price of $444.

Corrective Work: Practice corrections five times each.

LESSON 19

Aim: To learn
   Numbers: **1** and **5**
   Symbols: ! (**exclamation point**) and % (**percent**)
To build speed with **ble**
To develop sustained typing skill with five-minute timings

15   (25)   72   (82)

Single spacing

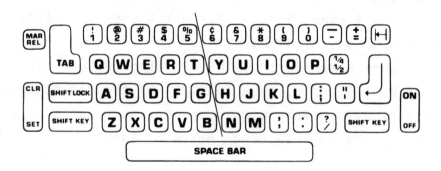

Warm-up: Type the drill once and the sentences five times each.

```
f4f  f$f  j7j  j&j  f4f  f$f  j7j  j&j  f4f  f$f  j7j  j&j  f4f  f$f
;-;  ;';  ;";  ;/;  ;?;  ;-;  ;';  ;";  ;/;  ;?;  ;-;  ;';  ;";  ;/;
```

Now is the time for all good men to come to the aid of
the party.

The quick brown fox jumped over the lazy dogs.

Skill-Building Work: ble

1. Type a line of **ble**, starting slowly and increasing speed. Type **ble** as a unit in the words following.

```
ble ble ble ble ble ble ble ble ble ble ble ble ble ble
able fable gable sable stable table cable capable
valuable

available movable lovable enjoyable liable horrible
possible impossible sensible visible invisible
responsible

suitable reasonable comfortable probable trouble
terrible treble foible credible incredible understandable

The capable nurse is sensible; she is responsible for
making the patient comfortable.

The repair on the valuable painting is hardly visible.
It is almost impossible to detect.  The cost is very
reasonable.
```

2. **Preview Practice—three times each**

```
important      accurately     accuracy      omitted
material       typographical     error       substitute
understanding     wrong      figure     proofreading
submits      women     tremendous     crowds     lawsuits
pending      if it is     will be     does not     $4,444
```

Double spacing

3. **Two One-Minute Timings, each followed by corrective work.**

```
                          5                        10
    It is just as important to learn to type numbers
                       15                        20
accurately as it is to type words.  In fact, accuracy
                     25                     29
in typing numbers is even more important.
```

Center the heading

ACCURACY IN TYPING NUMBERS

4. Two Five-Minute Timings, each followed by corrective work.

It is just as important to learn to type numbers
accurately as it is to type words. In fact, accuracy
in typing numbers is even more important.

If there is an error in the typing of a word or if
a letter is omitted, the error is obvious to the typist
as well as to any reader of the material. The typographical error practically leaps out of the print and
the correct spelling can be substituted. The error, in
most instances, does not interfere with the understanding
of the sentence even if the competence of the typist is
questionable.

However, if there is a wrong figure or an omitted
figure, there is no way that the reader can know it is
wrong. If a price is incorrectly typed on a bill and if
the typist has not corrected it when proofreading, a
customer will be overcharged or undercharged. It is
even worse if a figure is omitted. What happens when a
painter submits a bid for $74 when he meant $474?

Last year a newspaper ad from a large department

```
      195                              200
store advertised a mink coat for $444.  The crowds the
205                        210                      215
next morning were tremendous; women were hurt.  The
                          220                    225
price should have been $4,444.  Some lawsuits are still
      228
pending.
```

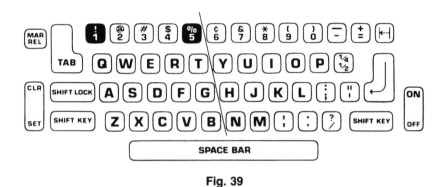

Fig. 39

Single spacing

New Keys 1 ! (Exclamation Point) and 5 % (Percent)
    1. The **A** finger controls 1 and !. Depress the right shift key for !.

Step 1—New Key Preview

While anchoring **F D S** fingers on their guide keys, reach up with the **A** finger to **Q** and above **Q** in the same direction to number **1**. Feel **a q 1 q a**. Feel **a q 1 a**. Feel **a 1 a** several times. Depress the right shift key and feel for **1**. You are now reaching **!**. Without the shift key, reach for **1**. With the shift key, reach for **!**.

(If your manual machine does not have a key for figure **1**, use lower case L for **1** (one). An exclamation point is made by striking ' (apostrophe), backspacing, and striking . (period). Practice ! ! !.

```
aqlqa aqlqa aqlqa aqla aqla aqla ala ala ala a!a a!a a!a
1 11 111 14 17 11,114 147,111 Oh! Oh! oh! oh! oh! oh!
```

Space **once** after an exclamation point if it is **within** a sentence. Space **twice** after an exclamation point at the **end** of a sentence.

```
What a hot day!  There are 174 people in the restaurant.
Oh! I am so happy to see that you saved $414 this month.
```

2. **5** and **%** are controlled by the **F** finger.

Step 1—New Key Preview

While anchoring **A S D** fingers on their guide keys, reach with the **F** finger for 4. Move from 4 to the right and your finger is on 5. Feel **f 4 5 f**. Feel 4, which is to the left of **F**. Feel 5, which is slightly to the right of **F**. Feel the reaches for **f 4 f f 5 f** until you are comfortable with both reaches.

Depress the right shift key and reach for 5. You are reaching for **%**. Without the shift key, reach for 5. With the shift key, reach for **%**. Memorize these keys while feeling for them.

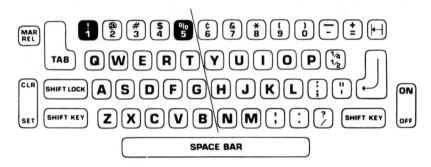

Step 2—New Key Tryout

```
f45f  f45f  f4f  f5f  f4f  f5f  f%f  f5f  f%f  f5f  f5f  f%f  f5f
5%  5%  5%  1%  15%  14%  7%  45%  41%  75%  54%  17%  51%  71%  57%
```

```
What a high price!  You can buy this radio for 15% less.
Do this arithmetic:  15% of $45; 75% of $17.45.
```

Self-Testing Work: **Part 1**

```
ala  a!a  f4f  f$f  f5f  f%f  j7j  j&j  ala  a!a  f4f  f$f  f5f  f%f
What a surprise!  All of the 15 guests are on time.
```

```
$1  $4  $5  $7  $41  $44  $45  $45.15  $5,547  $145  $711  $1,577
1%  4%  5%  7%  41%  44%  45%  57%  75%  51%  71%  17%  145%  51.4%
```

```
The hospital has 715 beds.  Only 415 are occupied.
Jacobs & Mason are having their annual sale.  Come early!
```

```
What a beautiful painting!  Who is the artist?
Oh! I had no idea that this is your work!
```

Double spacing

Type these paragraphs accurately.

Part 2

The exclamation point is used after words, phrases
or sentences to indicate surprise or strong emotion.
EXAMPLES: It's truly amazing! I don't believe it!
You must leave immediately!

Greene & Arnold have announced that their store
will be open until 5 o'clock Monday through Wednesday
and until 7 o'clock Thursday through Saturday. For
last minute shopping, the store will be open until
1 o'clock on the Sunday before Christmas.

Meet me at my office--room 145--at 4 o'clock,
Tuesday, April 17. Mr. Lazar, a reporter from the
"Sentinel," will be interviewing me about the new shop
we are opening under the name of Gold & Sons.

Wise & O'Brien are offering 15% discount on all
orders of $75 or more with cash payment. They offer
a discount of 5% for payment within 7 days. This offer
will be in effect until February 14. They must dispose
of $47,555 worth of merchandise to make room in their
warehouse for new stock arriving February 15.

We expect 17 cases of canned fruit to be delivered
today. Please have a check ready; the bill will be for
$75.14 less 5%.

Corrective Work: Practice each correction five times.

Challenge Work: Can you type a perfect copy of the following paragraph?

On April 14 Jones & Daniels are having a one-day
sale. Steel desks with formica tops will be sold for
$415, a saving of 17%. Desk chairs will be sold for
$75, a saving of 15%. Discontinued style lamps in
perfect condition will be sold at 45% discount. Come
early!

LESSON 20

Aim: To learn
     Numbers: **2** and **3**
     Symbols: **@** (**at**) and **#** (**number**)
  To build speed with **ter**
  To develop sustained typing skill with five-minute timings

15 (25)

                  72 (82)

Single spacing

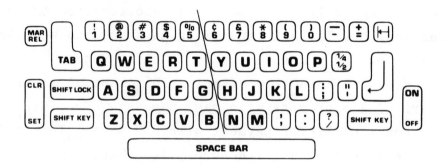

Warm-up: Type the drills as you say the letters. Type the sentence ten times.

```
ala a!a f4f f$f f5f f%f j7j j&j ala a!a f4f f$f j7j j&j
;-; ;-; ;'; ;'; ;"; ;"; ;/; ;/; ;?; ;?; ala f4f f5f j7j

I realize that C. & J.'s bill for $71 is discounted 5%.
```

Skill-Building Work: ter

  1. Type a line of **ter**, starting slowly and increasing speed. Type **ter** as a unit whether it appears at the beginning or end of a word.

```
ter ter ter ter ter ter ter ter ter ter ter ter ter ter
term term term term term term term term term term term

termite tern terminal terminate terrace territory terse
terrestrial terrible terrific terror terrorism terrier
```

later meter faster master roster disaster chapter luster
plaster poster semester adjuster Rochester winter cluster

painter daughter sister pointer jester writer typewriter
duster muster commuter computer adjuster yesterday

The spring semester seems to pass much faster than the
winter term during which we had terrible weather.

Mr. Foster of Rochester engaged the master painter
to paint portraits of his wife, sister, and daughter.

2. Preview Practice—three times each

importance		"decimal point."	omission	zeros
dollars	hundred	thousand	million	reverse
omitted	recently	depositor	corrected	
bookstore	clerk	is the	of this	that the

Double spacing

3. Two One-Minute Timings. You will find the same words repeated on succeeding
lines. Keep your eyes on the copy.

5   10
Just as the accuracy of a single figure in a number
15   20
is of prime importance, so is the tiny dot called a
25   30
"decimal point." The omission of this dot in front of
35   40
the two zeros which indicate no cents can change one
45   50
dollar into one hundred dollars or change one hundred
55   60
dollars into ten thousand dollars.

Practice corrections after each timing.

Center the heading

The Decimal Point

4. Two Five-Minute Timings

Just as the accuracy of a single figure in a number

is of prime importance, so is the tiny dot called a

"decimal point." The omission of this dot in front of

the two zeros which indicate no cents can change one

dollar into one hundred dollars or change one hundred

dollars into ten thousand dollars.

A bank recently sent a bank statement to a

depositor with a deposit of three million dollars

recorded. The man was delighted to find himself so

rich. But soon that little omitted dot was found.

The deposit was corrected to thirty thousand dollars.

The reverse also happened. A copy of a rare, old

book was sold by a bookstore clerk for four dollars

instead of four hundred dollars. He thought he saw a

decimal point.

When listing figures for addition, be sure that

the decimal points are accurately lined up, one under

the other.

NOTE: In all the lessons following, please remember to practice all corrections after each timing and to record your scores.

Recording your scores is a means of measuring your progress. Compare your scores not so much with the day before as with the week before. You will surely see improvement.

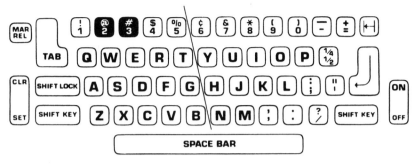

FIG. 40

New Keys: 2 @ (At) and 3 # (Number)
1. The **S** finger controls **2** and **@**. Depress the right shift for **@**.

MANUAL. You may find **@** to the right of the semicolon. Depress the left shift key for **@**. Your drill will be ; **@** ;

Step 1—New Key Preview

While anchoring D and F fingers on their guide keys, reach with the **S** finger to W and above W in the same direction to **2**. Feel s w **2** w s. Feel s w **2** s. Feel s **2** s several times.

Depress the right shift key and feel for **2**. You are now reaching for **@**.

Without the shift key, reach for **2**. With the shift key, reach for **@**. Memorize this.

Single spacing

Step 2—New Key Tryout

NOTE: Leave a space after **@**. Type the first two lines twice, the rest once.

```
sw2ws sw2ws sw2s sw2s s2s s2s s2s s@s s@s s@s s@s s@s
2 shirts @ $24.52.   12 blouses @ $27.   4 dresses @ $52.

Use @ to indicate the unit price when typing bills.
Use @ only with amount of money typed in figures.
```

2. The **D** finger controls **3** and **#** (number)

Step 1—New Key Preview

While anchoring the **F** finger on its guide key, reach with the **D** finger for **E** and above E in the same direction for **3**. (Some people are more comfortable anchoring on **A** and **S**.) Feel d e **3** e d. Feel d e **3** d. Feel d **3** d several times.

Depress the right shift key and feel for **3**. You are now reaching for **#**.

Without the shift key, feel for **3**. With the shift key, feel for **#**. Memorize this.

Step 2—New Key Tryout

NOTE: There is no space between # and the figure that follows.
Type the first two lines twice, the rest once.

```
de3ed de3ed de3d de3d d3d d3d d3d d3d d#d d#d d#d d#d
#3 needles; #3 needles; #12 brushes; #12 brushes;

31 32 33 34 35 37 21 22 23 24 25 27 13 23 33 43 53 73
#3 brooms @ $3; #12 brushes @ $34; #1 #2 #3 #4 #5 #7
Space after @ and &.  Do not space after # and $.
```

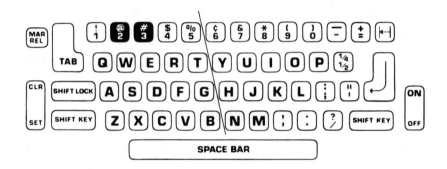

Self-Testing Work:

Part 1

```
s2s s@s d3d d#d s2s s@s d3d d#d s2s s@s d3d d#d s2s
Track #3, Track #2, Track #1, Track #33, Track #32

Order #3, Order #2, Order #1, Order #33, Order #32
Send a bill to Baker & Co. for 23 #742 chairs @ $53.15.

12 boxes of #73 @ $42; 23 pairs of #52 @ $74.54.
15 dozen of #51 @ $23; 754 sheets @ $14.75.

We are shipping your order #573.  It amounts to $352.11.
We billed you for 125 boxes of #14 cards @ $5.75.
```

Part 2

Type the following paragraphs in *single spacing*. When typing paragraphs in single spacing, always leave an extra line space between paragraphs. In other words, RETURN twice.

```
     On February 23, Stanton & Abrams are moving their
offices from 1314 Broadway to 752 Atlantic Avenue.  Their
new telephone numbers will be 372-313 and 372-314.
```

Through an error you sent us 35 cassettes #543
@ $3.45 instead of 35 cassettes #435 @ $4.55. They
arrived on November 14; they were shipped from your warehouse on November 12. Will you please have your truck
call and make the exchange.

Corrective Work: Be sure to practice all corrections.

Double spacing

Challenge Work: Aim at perfect work.

If you are in a high tax bracket, you might be
interested in investing in Municipal Bonds which yield
a rate of 7% and more. Usually the longer the term before maturity, the higher the rate. Because the interest
on Municipal Bonds is free of taxes, 7% may be the
equivalent of 14% taxable interest for you. If you have
any questions, phone us at 512-7172.

LESSON 21

Aim: To learn
      Numbers: **6** and **8**
      Symbols: **¢** (**cents**) and ***** (**asterisk**)
  To increase speed with **sh**
  To develop skill with five-minute timings

15 (25)

72 (82)

Single spacing

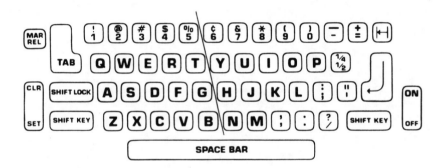

Warm-up: Close your eyes and type the alphabet twice. After the drills, type each sentence five times.

```
abcdefghijklmnopqrstuvwxyz abcdefghijklmnopqrstuvwxyz

ala a!s s2s s@s d3d d#d f4f f$f f5f f%f j7j j&j
ala a!s s2s s@s d3d d#d f4f f$f f5f f%f j7j j&j

The invoice billed 3 dozen #23 cartons @ $3.25.
The quick brown fox jumped over the lazy dogs.
```

Skill-Building Work: sh

1. Type a line of **sh**, starting slowly and increasing speed. Type **sh** as a unit.

```
sh sh sh sh sh sh sh sh sh sh sh sh sh sh sh sh sh sh
ship ship ship ship ship ship ship ship ship ship ship

she should shall shake shell shame shower shave shove
shoe shack shock shop shape shawl shoot shine shed show

wash wish flash flush rash trash brash sash lash clash
fish hash cash crash crush mash swish dish dash squash

Ship the fresh fish by air; otherwise freeze it.
Shall I put a dash of pepper on the shellfish?

Use the electric beater to mix the butter in the batter.
Shell the nuts; then crush and mash them with caramel.
She should shop for the shoes and shawl with cash.
```

2. **Preview Practice—three times each**

```
slowly      touch      numbers     symbols     tempted
practice    whenever    besides     proficiency
facility    once       keyboard    especially     may be
to do      in the     you will
```

Double spacing

3. **Two One-Minute Timings**

```
                         5
      You may be tempted to look at your fingers when
10                        15                        20
typing numbers and symbols.  If you do, it will slow
                      25                      30
you down.  Think how slowly you would be typing now if
                  35                      40
you had to look at your fingers for the letters instead
              45                  49
of typing them by touch, as you do.
```

Center the heading
```
      TOUCH TYPING OF NUMBERS AND SYMBOLS
```

4. Two Five-Minute Timings

REMINDER: If you should finish before the time is up, start again from the beginning.

```
                              5
         You may be tempted to look at your fingers when
10                           15                          20
typing numbers and symbols.  If you do, it will slow
                    25                      30
you down.  Think how slowly you would be typing now if
                35                      40
you had to look at your fingers for the letters instead
            45                      50
of typing them by touch as you do.  The same is true
        55
with numbers and symbols.
                    60                          65
         Whenever you look away from your copy, you must
        70                          75
find your place again.  Besides losing time, you might
    80                          85
go back to a wrong line, especially if a word or a
    90                      95
number is repeated in the copy.
                        100                          105
         If you will spend the time and make the effort now
                    110                         115
to learn to make full use of all the keys on the key-
                120                         125
board, you will save hours and hours of time in the
                130                         135
future.  Once you learn to touch type with proficiency
        140                     145
and ease, the skill will remain with you for all your
        150
lifetime.
```

New Keys 6 ¢ (Cents) and 8 * (Asterisk)

1. The **J** finger controls **6** and **¢**. Depress the left shift key for **¢**.

MANUAL: The **¢** key is to the right of semicolon. **¢** is on the same key as **@**. No shift key is needed for **¢**. The shift key is needed for **@**. Your drill will be ; ¢ ; ; @ ;.

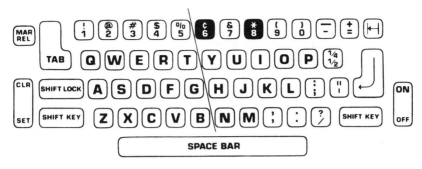

Fig. 41

Step 1—New Key Preview

While keeping **; L K** fingers on the guide keys, reach with the **J** finger for **Y** and above **Y** in the same direction for **6**. Feel **j y 6 y j**. Feel **j y 6 j**. Feel **j 6 j**. Feel **j 7 6 j**. Feel **j 7 j   j 6 j** until each reach feels comfortable.

Depress the left shift key and feel for **6**. You are now touching **¢** (cents).

Without the shift key, feel for **6**. With the shift key feel for **¢**. Memorize this.

Single spacing

Step 1—New Key Tryout

NOTE: Leave no space between the number and the cents sign.

Type the first two lines twice, the rest once.

```
jy6yj jy6yj jy6j jy6j j6j j6j j6j j6j j¢j j¢j j¢j j¢j
6¢ 16¢ 26¢ 36¢ 46¢ 56¢ 66¢ 76¢ 61¢ 62¢ 63¢ 64¢ 65¢ 66¢

j6j j7j j6j j7j j6j j7j j6j j¢j j&j j¢j j&j j¢j j&j j¢j
The candy bar costs 36¢.   The pen costs 75¢.
Send 76 streamers @ 26¢ and 56 favors @ 67¢.
```

2. The **K** finger controls the key for **8** and ***** (**asterisk**).

MANUAL: You may find ***** on the same key as the hyphen. Your drill will be **; - ;   ; * ;**.

Step 1—New Key Preview

While anchoring **;** and **L** fingers on the guide keys, reach with the **K** finger for **I** and above **I** in the same direction for **8**. Feel **k i 8 i k**. Feel **k i 8 k**. Feel **k 8 k** several times.

Depress the left shift key and feel for **8**. You are now touching *****.

Without the shift key, feel for **8**. With the shift key, feel for *****.

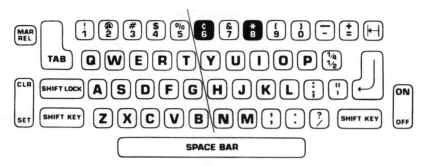

Fig. 41

Step 2—New Key Tryout

NOTE: Leave no space between * and the word it accompanies.

Type the first two lines twice, the rest once.

```
ki8ik ki8ik ki8k ki8k k8k k8k k8k k8k k*k k*k k*k k*k
81 82 83 84 85 86 87 8¢ 18¢ 28¢ 38¢ 48¢ 58¢ 68¢ 78¢ 88¢

k8k k*k k8k k*k k8k k*k k8k k*k k8k k*k k8k k*k k8k k*k
```

In this report, all Middle East countries mentioned
are designated by an asterisk: Egypt*, England, France,
Iran*, Iraq*, Israel*, Italy, Jordan*, Lebanon*, Saudi
Arabia*, Syria*.

Self-Testing Work: **Part 1**

```
ala a!a s2s s@s d3d d#d f4f f$f f5f f%f j6j j¢j j7j j&j
k8k k*k j6j j¢j k8k k*k j6j j¢j k8k k*k j6j j¢j k8k k*k
```

Soap @ 65¢; Muffins @ 68¢; Oranges @ 25¢; Bananas @ 17¢;
Bread @ 87¢; Pears @ 21¢; Apples @ 18¢; Scallions @ 36¢;

Our price on notebooks is down from 78¢ to 68¢.
Please deduct 18¢ as a 5% cash discount from $3.65.

                    Part 2   *Double spacing*

Use * in the body of an article or tabulation to
indicate reference to a footnote. In an article or
tabulation, * is written after the word or number, with
no space between. In a footnote, * is written before
the footnote with no space between.

In order to accommodate our working customers, we have extended our banking hours. On Monday through Thursday our bank will stay open until 6 p.m. On Friday our bank will stay open until 8 p.m.

At one time it was possible to buy a candy bar, a subway ride, or even a cigar with 5¢. A 25¢ coin could admit a person to the movies or to the second balcony of a theater. However, these prices should be evaluated in relation to the average earnings of a worker. A salesperson or an office worker would have received $15 as a week's pay in those days.

Corrective Work: Practice all corrections five times.

Challenge Work: Keep your eyes on the book. If you hesitate about the placement of a number or symbol, refer to the keyboard chart, not to your machine keyboard.

Find the cost of the following: 156 lbs. Butter @ 87¢; 145 doz. Eggs @ 85¢; 172 boxes Oranges @ $14.15; 364 cans California Canned Peaches @ 48¢; 186 cans #1 Campbell's Soup @ 24¢.

LESSON 22

Aim: To learn
      Numbers: **9** and **0**
      Symbols: ( ) (**parentheses**)
   To build speed with **ck**
   To develop sustained typing skill with five-minute timings

15 (25)

72 (82)

Single spacing

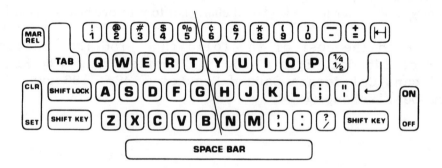

Warm-up: Type the drills once and the sentences five times each. Remember to say the drills as you type them.

```
aqaza swsxs dedcd frftfgfbfvf jujyjhjnjmj kik,k lol.l
;p;/; ;?; ;'; ;"; ;-; ala a!a s2s s@s d3d d#d f4f f$f
f5f f%f j6j j¢j j7j j&j k8k k*k 1 2 3 4 5 6 7 8 j¢j k*k
```

The imitation stones sell for 86¢, the genuine for $865.
Zelda quickly mixed the very big jar of new soap flakes.

Skill-Building Work: ck
  1. Type a line of **ck**, starting slowly and increasing speed. Type **ck** as a unit.

ck ck ck ck ck ck ck ck ck ck ck ck ck ck ck ck ck ck
check check check check check check check check check

stock truck tack track tick stick stack stuck back buck
sack crack clock knock pluck hack shack Jack wick tuck

lack slack quack quick struck sock frock dock package
deck pack pick peck speck wreck crock neck luck hock

    The clock struck twelve. There was a knock on the
door. Zack plucked up courage to open the door a crack.

    The sailor was quick to pick up the rock that struck
the deck. Luckily, the rock did not crack the deck.

    Jack gave a check to the truck driver for the
package. Jack's stock is up to date.

2. Preview Practice—three times each; more if you need it.

dictionary   "parentheses"   expression   whole
curved   clearness   without   altering   additions
often   illustrations   definitions   information
"parenthesis"   singular   sentences   quotation

Double spacing

3. Two One-Minute Timings

                   5
    The dictionary describes "parentheses" as two
  10   15   20
curved lines which set off an expression. Just like
                   25   29
quotation marks, parentheses come in pairs.

Center the title

                    PARENTHESES

4. Two Five-Minute Timings

$$\overset{5}{}$$
The dictionary describes "parentheses" as two

$$\overset{10}{}\qquad\qquad\qquad\overset{15}{}\qquad\qquad\qquad\overset{20}{}$$
curved lines which set off an expression. Just like

$$\overset{25}{}$$
quotation marks, parentheses come in pairs.

$$\overset{30}{}\qquad\qquad\qquad\overset{35}{}$$
Parentheses are used in writing to enclose words,

$$\overset{40}{}\qquad\qquad\qquad\overset{45}{}$$
figures, phrases or whole sentences that add to the

$$\overset{50}{}\qquad\qquad\qquad\overset{55}{}\qquad\qquad\qquad\overset{60}{}$$
clearness of a statement without altering its meaning.

$$\overset{65}{}\qquad\qquad\qquad\overset{70}{}$$
These additions are often illustrations, definitions

$$\overset{75}{}\qquad\qquad\qquad\overset{80}{}$$
or added information thrown in for good measure. Pa-

$$\overset{85}{}\qquad\qquad\qquad\overset{90}{}$$
rentheses are used to enclose figures, following the

$$\overset{95}{}\qquad\qquad\qquad\overset{100}{}$$
spelling out of those figures. When listing items in

$$\overset{105}{}\qquad\qquad\qquad\overset{110}{}$$
an outline, parentheses are often used around letters

$$\overset{115}{}$$
or numbers.

$$\overset{120}{}\qquad\qquad\qquad\overset{125}{}$$
The singular of "parentheses" is "parenthesis."

The material in today's timings is much more difficult than in previous timings. It requires concentration. Don't be disappointed if your score is lower today.

New Keys 9 ((Left Parenthesis) and 0) (Right Parenthesis)
1. The **L** finger controls **9** and **(** (left parenthesis). Depress the left shift key for (.

Step 1—New Key Preview

While touching **J** and **K** fingers to their guide keys, reach with the **L** finger for **O** and above **O** in the same direction for **9**. Feel **l o 9 o l**. Feel **l o 9 l**. Feel **l 9 l** several times.

Depress the left shift key and reach for **9**. You are now touching **(** (left parenthesis). Without the shift key, feel for **9**. With the shift key, reach for **(**.

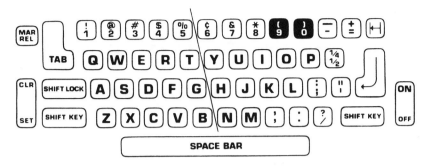

Fig. 42

Single spacing

Step 2—New Key Tryout

Type the first two lines twice, the rest once.

```
1o9o1 1o9o1 1o91 1o91 191 191 191 191 1(1 1(1 1(1 1(1
91 92 93 94 95 96 97 98 99 19 29 39 49 59 69 79 89 99

191 1(1 191 1(1 191 1(1 191 1(1 191 1(1 191 1(1 191 1(1
$4.99 $29.79 $954.85 9% 19% 93% 69% 69¢ 89¢ #39 #69 #59

Place my order for 19 boxes of envelopes @ $2.49.
My telephone number has been changed to 791-9834.
```

2. The **semi** finger controls **0** and **)** (right parenthesis). Depress the left shift key for).

Step 1—New Key Preview

While anchoring **J K L** fingers on the guide keys, reach with the **;** finger for **P** and above **P** in the same direction for **)**. Feel **; p 0 p ;**. Feel **; p 0 ;**. Feel **; 0 ;** several times.

Depress the shift key and reach for **0**. You are now on **)**.

Without the shift key, feel for **0**. With the shift key, feel for **)**. Memorize these reaches.

Step 2—New Key Tryout

Type the first two lines twice, the rest once.

```
;p0p; ;p0p; ;p0; ;p0; ;0; ;0; ;0; ;0; ;); ;); ;); ;);
10 20 30 40 50 60 70 80 90 100 1,000 2,000 3,000 4,000

191 1(1 ;0; ;); 191 1(1 ;0; ;); 191 1(1 ;0; ;); 191 1(1
(1) (2) (3) (4) (5) (6) (7) (8) (9) (10) (20) (30) (40)

     We require a deposit of one hundred dollars ($100)
on the desk you ordered for nine hundred dollars ($900).
```

Self-Testing Work: **Part 1**

```
ala a!a s2s s@s d3d d#d f4f f$f f5f f%f j6j j¢j j7j j&j
k8k k*k 191 1(1 ;0; ;); 191 1(1 ;0; ;); 191 1(1 ;0; ;);
```

```
Jones's order #901 (dated March 30) has been shipped.
Our check #786 (dated April 9) was sent on April 10.
```

```
Closeout!  One thousand (1,000) paperback books @ 79¢.
Introductory offer!  Join the LITERARY GUILD.
Choose four best-sellers for two dollars ($2.00).
```

```
American Airlines, Flight #321 (New York to Chicago).
United Airlines, Flight #25 (New York to San Francisco).
Pan American Airlines, Flight #1 (Around the World).
```

                       Part 2   *Double spacing*

```
     Charter flights at off-season rates are available
from New York to Europe (Copenhagen or Amsterdam), from
Miami to the Caribbean (Jamaica or Curacao), from San
Francisco to the Orient (Singapore, Thailand, and Hong
Kong).
     To be placed on our free mailing list, please
(1) write us on your office stationery
(2) indicate the nature of your business
(3) mail your request to our nearest office.
     The contract specified (a) 12 boxes to a carton;
(b) cartons fastened by wire bands; (c) complete delivery
by September 10.
```

Corrective Work: Practice corrections.

Challenge Work: Now that you have learned all the numbers on the keyboard, try to type a perfect copy of this memorandum.

```
     On November 19 I expect to leave Chicago (O'Hare)
at 10:05 a.m. (CST) and arrive in New York (La Guardia)
at 1:00 p.m. (EST).  My flight is #322 on TWA.  I have
reserved a room at the Palace Hotel for three nights.

     Please leave a message for me as to when and where
we can meet either in the afternoon of November 19 or
the morning of November 20.
```

LESSON 23

Aim: To learn
    Fractions ½ (**one half**) and ¼ (**one quarter**)
    Made fractions
  To increase speed with **ight** and five-minute timings

15 (25)

72 (82)

Single spacing

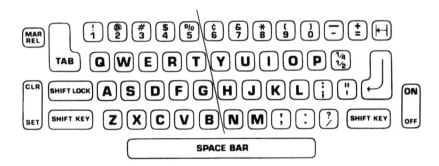

Warm-up: Remember to say the drills as you type them. Type the drills twice and the sentences five times each.

```
al!a s2@s d3#d f4$f f5%f j6¢j j7&j k8*k l9(l ;0); ;'";
We sent the $900 for the copier (Canon) on September 16.

The quick brown fox jumped over the lazy dogs.
```

Skill-Building Work: ight

  1. Type a line of **ight**. Type **ight** as a unit.

```
ight ight ight ight ight ight ight ight ight ight ight
right right right right right right right right right

sight light fight fright tight night might blight slight
bright plight alight delight sunlight starlight flight

straight lightning enlighten height weight freight
Record your height and weight on the doctor's chart.
```

105

This package is slightly overweight for parcel post. Pack it tightly and send it by freight.

In the desert the silvery light of moonlight is almost as bright as the yellow light of sunlight. At night under a full moon one might read a book.

2. Preview Practice—each word and phrase three times.

```
position     important    posture     accurately
prevent      fatigue      center      chair      erect
loosely      elbows       curve       naturally     wrists
relax        of the       with the    on the
```

Double Spacing

3. Two One-Minute Timings

```
                          5                         10
        Your position at the typewriter is more important
                     15                       20
than you think.  Good posture will help you type more
                 25                       30
accurately and faster.  Good posture will help prevent
           33
fatigue.
```

Center this heading

PROPER POSITION AT THE MACHINE

4. Two Five-Minute Timings

```
                          5                         10
        Your position at the typewriter is more important
                     15                       20
than you think.  Good posture will help you type more
                 25                       30
accurately and faster.  Good posture will help prevent

fatigue.
             35                         40
        Follow these simple rules for good posture:  Sit
       45                   50
in front of the machine with the center of your body in
```

<pre>
                    55   60
front of the letter J. In a chair that gives you proper
               65   70
support, sit erect with your hips well back. Keep both
          75   80
feet flat on the floor with one foot a little ahead
     85   90   95
of the other. Your arms should hang loosely with your
                         100   110
elbows close to your body. Curve your fingers naturally.
                    115   120
Keep your wrists low without touching the machine.

                    125
Learn to relax.

                              130
     Place your copy material to the right of your
135   140   145
machine. Once having checked that your fingers are on
                         150   155
the proper guide keys, keep your eyes on the copy.
</pre>

NOTE: Reread this exercise for content.

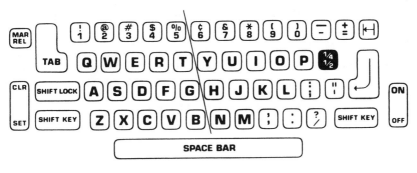

Fig. 43

New Key   Fractions ½ and ¼

The fractions ½ and ¼ are controlled by the ; finger.   Depress the left shift key for ¼.

Step 1—New Key Preview

While keeping **J K L** fingers on the guide keys, reach with the ; finger up and to the right.   You will be feeling ½.   Feel the difference in reach for **P** and ½.   Feel ; ½ ; ; **p** ;.   Feel ; ½ ; several times.

Depress the left shift key and reach for ¼.

Without the shift key, reach for ½.   With the shift key, reach for ¼.   Memorize these keys.

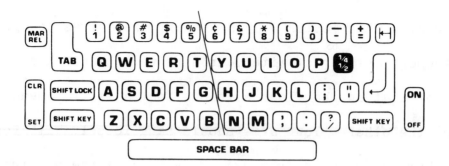

Single spacing

Step 2—New Key Tryout

There is **no** space between a number and fractions ½ and ¼.

;½; ;¼; ;½; ;¼; ;½; ;¼; ;½; ;¼; ;½; ;¼; ;½; ;¼; ;½; ;¼;
12½ 12¼ 13½ 13¼ 14½ 14¼ 15½ 15¼ 16½ 16¼ 17½ 17¼ 18½ 18¼

;p; ;½; ;p; ;½; ;p; ;½; ;p; ;½; ;p; ;½; ;p; ;½; ;p; ;½;
Peaches @ 54½¢; Peaches @ 54½¢; Peaches @ 54½¢; 6 @ 54½¢

Pears @ 63¼¢; Pears @ 63¼¢; Pears @ 63¼¢; Pears @ 63¼¢
The office measures 15½ feet by 10¼ feet.

Made fractions. Fractions other than ½ and ¼ are typed with the / (diagonal).

New Work Tryout

1/5 2/9 4/9 2/3 1/8 5/7 1/6 7/9 3/4 7/9 5/8 1/8 5/6

When a **made fraction** follows a whole number, leave a space between the whole number and the made fraction.

3 1/8, 10 3/4, 25 5/6, 34 8/9, 46 3/8, 26 7/8, 6 2/7

Self-Testing Work: **Part 1**

12 boxes @ 10¼¢; 36 Pairs @ 49½¢; 15 dozen @ 59¼¢
17 doz. @ 68 3/8; 5 boxes @ 89 1/6; 4 sets @ $3.75;

By saving 1½¢ on each box (#9), we'll make a profit.
Can you shave ¼ inch from the width of the counter?

For measurements following figures, ' represents feet.
Similarly, " stands for inches.

The rug must be exactly 20½ feet by 14 3/4 feet.
The rug must be exactly 20' 6" x 14' 9".

Buy now! #78 are reduced to 12¼¢; #96 to 76½¢.
Astor & Sons are selling blankets (Arista) at 6% off.

The large painting requires a frame 5' 3" x 2' 10".
Without your calculator, can you figure 7/8 of 288?

Part 2   *Double spacing*

Some common fractions and their equivalent in per
cent are listed here: ½ is 50%; ¼ is 25%; 1/3 is 33 1/3%;
2/3 is 66 2/3%; 1/5 is 20%; 2/5 is 40%; 3/5 is 60%;
4/5 is 80%; 1/6 is 16 2/3%; 5/6 is 83 1/3%; 1/7 is
14 2/7%; 2/7 is 28 4/7%; 3/7 is 42 6/7%; 4/7 is 57 1/7%;
5/7 is 71 3/7%; 6/7 is 85 5/7%; 1/8 is 12½%; 3/8 is
37½%; 5/8 is 62½%; 7/8 is 87½%.

Corrective Work: Practice corrections five times.

Challenge Work: Try to type a perfect copy.

As we all know, Abraham Lincoln was born in 1809
in Kentucky. His father could not read or write until
after his marriage to Nancy Hanks. .Abe's mother
was a woman of exceptional intellect and character.
It was she who taught Abraham to read and write. His
entire schooling in an ABC school was less than
a year. But he was a voracious reader. He had few
books, but he knew Shakespeare, Burns, a life of
Washington, and a history of the United States well.

LESSON 24

Aim: To complete the keyboard by learning the symbols __ (**underscore**), = (**equals**), and + (**plus**)
To learn how to type arithmetical signs for **multiplication**, **subtraction**, and **division**.
To increase speed with **qu** and timings

15 (25)

72 (82)

Single spacing

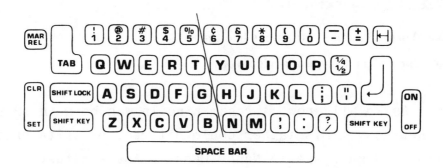

Warm-up: Say the drill as you type it.   Type each sentence five times.

al!a s2@s d3#d f4$f f5%f j6¢j j7&j k8*k 19(1 ;0); ;−;
;$\frac{11}{24}$; ;'"; ;/?; ;$\frac{1}{2}$; ;$\frac{1}{4}$; ;$\frac{1}{2}$; ;$\frac{1}{4}$; ;$\frac{1}{2}$; ;$\frac{1}{4}$; ;$\frac{1}{2}$; ;$\frac{1}{4}$; ;$\frac{1}{2}$; ;$\frac{1}{4}$;

Today our stock rose from 19$\frac{1}{4}$ to 20$\frac{1}{2}$.

The quick brown fox jumped over the lazy dogs.

Now is the time for all good men to come to the aid of
the party.

Skill-Building Work: qu

1. Type a line of **qu**. Type **qu** as a unit.

```
qu qu qu qu qu qu qu qu qu qu qu qu qu qu qu qu qu qu
quart quart quart quart quart quart quart quart quart

quantity quality quarter quarrel quake qualify queen
question queue quick quiet quite quilt quaint quote

quit quire quirk quiver quiz queer quotation quill
The office manager requested 12 quires of paper.
A glutton requests quantity; a gourmet requests quality.

     The doctor quickly prescribed quinine and quiet for
the malaria patient.  We did not question his diagnosis.
He was quite sure.
```

2. **Preview Practice—three times each.**

```
evaluate      technique      recommended      experts
anchor      pivot      necessary      downward      inward
rounded      shorten      sacrifice      definitely
movements      avoid      elbow      relax      curve
naturally      do not      it is      with the      may have
on the      of the
```

Double spacing

3. **Two One-Minute Timings**

```
                          5                         10
     It is now time to evaluate your typing technique.
                     15
The rules following are recommended by experts.
     20                    25                        30
     Anchor both hands on the guide keys and pivot them
               33
when necessary.
```

Center the heading

```
                YOUR TYPING TECHNIQUE
```

4. Two Five-Minute Timings

5   10

It is now time to evaluate your typing technique.

15

The rules following are recommended by experts.

20   25   30

Anchor both hands on the guide keys and pivot them

when necessary.

35   40

Tap the center of the keys lightly and quickly

45   50

with the cushion of the curved fingers. Some experts

55   60

suggest a downward and inward motion.

65   70

It is just as important to release the key quickly

75

as to strike it quickly.

80   85

If your fingernails are long, you will find that

90   95

they do not permit you to strike the key with the

100   105

rounded tips of your fingers. You may have to shorten

110   115

them even if it is a sacrifice; otherwise they may break.

120   125

Long fingernails will definitely slow your typing.

130   135

Tap the key with finger movements only. Avoid

140   145

hand, wrist, arm, and elbow motions.

150   155

Keep your eyes on your copy even when striking

160

the RETURN key or returning the carriage.

165   170

Before starting to type, drop your hands to your

175   180   185

sides to relax them. Your fingers will curve naturally.

It is not expected that you will complete this exercise in five minutes at this time. However, read it to the end for content.

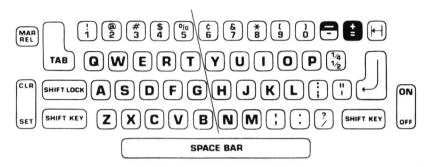

Fig. 44

New Keys　__ (Underscore)
　　　　　　 = (Equals)
　　　　　　 + (Plus)

__ (underscore) is controlled by the ; finger.　The underscore is on the same key as the - (hyphen) with the left shift key depressed.

Step 1—New Key Preview

Reach for - (hyphen) with the ; finger.　Depress the left shift key; you are reaching for the __ (underscore).　Feel ; - ;　; __ ; until it is familiar.　Memorize it.

MANUAL:

If you have a MANUAL typewriter, the **underscore** is on the 6 key with the left shift key depressed.　The drill will be j6__j j6j j__j.

For your MANUAL typewriter, make a copy of the following drills.　Keep them with this book.　Substitute them for the warm-up drills which are based on the electric and electronic keyboard.　The drills for the letters are the same.　The variation is in the symbols.

MANUAL KEYBOARD

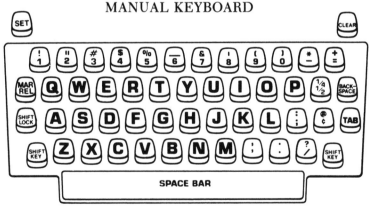

```
aqaza swsxs dedcd frftfgfbfvf jujyjhjnjmj kik,k lol.l
;p;/;
ala a!a s2s s"s d3d d#d f4f f$f f5f f%f j6j j_j j7j j&j
k8k k'k 191 1(1 ;0; ;); ;-; ;*; ;½; ;¼; ;¢; ;@; ;/; ;?;
```

If your machine has the [±] key, add ;=; ;+;.

To **underscore**:
1. Type the word or phrase. *Do not* RETURN.
2. **Backspace** for each letter in the material to be underscored. One method is to spell out the word or words as you backspace.
   If your machine has a **repeat backspacer**, hold it down until you reach the first letter.
3. Strike the shift lock.
4. Strike the **underscore** as you spell the words again.

Do not underscore beyond the letters.

If your machine has a REPEAT key, strike the **underscore** once; then hold down the REPEAT key for the rest of the underscoring. Again, do not underscore beyond the letters to be underscored.

Some electronic machines have an **automatic underscore** which underscores as you type. Consult your typewriter manual about its operation.

Single spacing

Step 2—New Key Tryout

```
;-; ;_; ;-; ;_; ;-; ;_; ;-; ;_; ;-; ;_; ;-; ;_; ;-; ;_;
This is a one-day sale.  All winter stock is half price.

Underscore for emphasis.  Underscore for emphasis.
Show italics on the typewriter by underscoring.
```

Double spacing

```
     On most electric and electronic typewriters, the
space bar and backspacer are repeat keys.  If you hold
on to either of these keys while depressing it, it will
rapidly repeat the forward or backward movement.
     Especially make use of the repeat process of the
backspacer when underscoring more than a few letters.
Be sure that you stop as if to type over the first
letter.
```

Here are two styles of underscoring:
Always Be Alert.
Always Be Alert.

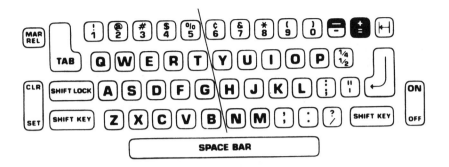

= (equals) and **+** (plus) are controlled by the **semi** finger. Depress the left shift key for **+** .

Step 1—New Key Preview

While anchoring fingers on to **J K L**, reach with ; finger for ½ and above in the same direction to the right for **=** . Feel ; ½ = ½ ;. Feel ; ½ = ;. Feel ; = ;. Feel the difference between ; - ; and ; = ;. Feel ; 0 ; ; - ; ; = ;. Again feel ; = ; several times.

Depress the left shift key and reach for **=** . You are now ready to strike **+** . Feel ; = + ;. Feel ; = ; ; + ;. Memorize these two symbols.

If, on a MANUAL machine, you do not find an equal sign or a plus sign on your keyboard you can type an **equal sign** by

(a) striking the hyphen
(b) backspacing once
(c) depressing the left shift very slightly and striking the hyphen again.

Practice this several times until you are satisfied with the equal sign.

You can type a **plus sign** by

(a) striking the hyphen
(b) backspacing once
(c) striking the diagonal.

The plus sign will look like this: +.

Step 2—New Key Tryout

;½=½; ;½=½; ;½=; ;½=; ;=; ;=; ;=; ;=; ;+; ;+; ;+;
10 + 20 = 30.   30 + 40 + 50 = 120.   120 + 150 = 270.

35 men + 26 women registered.   35 + 26 = 61 voters.
1 + 2 + 4 + 8 + 16 + 32 + 64 + 128 + 256 = 511.

REMINDER: Leave a space before and after an arithmetical symbol.

Other arithmetical symbols

(a) For **multiplication**, use lowercase **x**.
(b) For **subtraction**, use hyphen (-).
(c) For **division**, type colon (:), **backspace** and type hyphen (-). Thus ÷.

Arithmetical Tryout

```
18 times 10 divided by five minus 12 equals 24.
18 x 10 ÷ 5 - 12 = 24.   18 x 10 ÷ 5 - 12 = 24.

24 + 96 x 16 - 28 ÷ 4 = 473.   12 + 18 ÷ 3 = 10.
73 - 29 = 44.   75 ÷ 6 = 12½;.   92 x 12 = 1,104.
```

TIP: If you hesitate in typing numbers, type numbers from 1 to 100. Now close your eyes and repeat. You will soon feel comfortable with the figures.

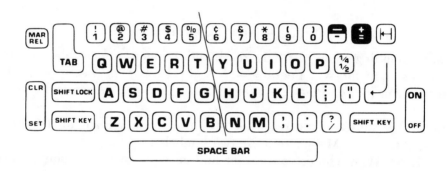

Self-Testing Work: **Part 1**

```
;-; ;_; ;=; ;+; ;-; ;_; ;=; ;+; ;-; ;_; ;=; ;+;
Order the New York Times and The Wall Street Journal.
To take advantage of our offer, reply by return mail.

     Let us divide the cost of this meal:  $65 + $3.25
tax = $68.25.  With the wine, the cost is $95.  $95 ÷ 3
= $31.67.

     Within the United States, it is not necessary to
write Air Mail on first-class mail.  It is necessary on
mail to a foreign country.

     Write a check to pay for the office rug that was
delivered today.  The bill is for $980 plus 8¼% tax, less
6% if paid within ten days:

$980 x .06 = $58.80 discount.  $980 - $58.80 = $921.20.
$921.20 x .0825 = $76 tax.  $921.20 + $76 = $997.20.
```

Double spacing

Part 2

The United States Post Office offers <u>Express</u> mail.
If an envelope (up to two pounds in weight) is brought
to the post office before 5 o'clock, it will be delivered
anywhere in the United States the next day before 3 p.m.

<u>First-class</u> mail consists of <u>written matter</u> (letters
and post cards).

<u>Second-class</u> mail consists of <u>newspapers</u> and <u>mag-
azines</u>, mailed in bulk and registered with the post
office.

<u>Third-class</u> mail consists of <u>small packages</u> (less
than 16 ounces in weight) which contain merchandise or
printed matter.

<u>Fourth-class</u> mail (also known as <u>Parcel Post</u>) con-
sists of packages from 16 ounces to 70 pounds. The meas-
urement of girth plus length must not exceed 108 inches.

Corrective Work: Practice corrected words or numbers five times.

LESSON 25

Aim: To learn to make **corrections**
To develop skill with timings

15 (25)

72 (82)

Single spacing

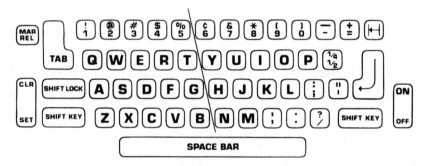

Warm-up: Say the drills as you type them.   Type the sentence five times.

abcdefghijklmnopqrstuvwxyz abcdefghijklmnopqrstuvwxyz
aqaza swsxs dedcd frftfgfbfvf jujyjhjnjmj kik,k lol.l
;p;/; al!a s2@s d3#d f4$f f5%f j6¢j j7&j k8*k l9(l ;0);
;−_; ;=+; ;¼; ;'"; ;/?; ;−_; ;=+; ;¼; ;'"; ;/?;

Now is the time for all good men to come to the aid of
the party.

Skill-Building Work

1. Preview Practice—three times each.

characters	occasional	mistake	corrections
immediately	undetectable	proofreading	
sophisticated	device	liquid	erasing
preferred			

Double spacing

2. Two One-Minute Timings

5   10

Since you have learned all the characters on the

118

¹⁵ ²⁰
keyboard and can type them by touch, you are now ready

²⁵ ³⁰
to learn how to correct errors. Even the best typist

³⁵ ³⁷
makes an occasional error.

Center the heading

CORRECTIONS

3. Two Five-Minute Timings

⁵ ¹⁰
Since you have learned all the characters on the

¹⁵ ²⁰
keyboard and can type them by touch, you are now ready

²⁵ ³⁰
to learn how to correct errors. Even the best typist

³⁵ ⁴⁰
makes an occasional error. Always remember, however,

⁴⁵ ⁵⁰
that it takes longer to correct an error than to type.

⁵⁵ ⁶⁰
When you type, you surely feel immediately when

⁶⁵ ⁷⁰
you strike the wrong key. This is the time to make the

⁷⁵ ⁸⁰ ⁸⁵
correction. If you did not detect the error immediately,

⁹⁰ ⁹⁵
it is still easy to correct while the paper is in the

¹⁰⁰ ¹⁰⁵
machine. Never remove a paper from the machine without

¹¹⁰ ¹¹⁵
carefully proofreading it first. If the correction is

¹²⁰ ¹²⁵ ¹³⁰
undetectable, the page will not have to be retyped.

¹³⁵ ¹⁴⁰
Most electric and electronic machines have correc-

¹⁴⁵ ¹⁵⁰
tion devices built in. Even if you use a manual type-

¹⁵⁵ ¹⁶⁰
writer, you are no longer dependent on an eraser for

¹⁶⁵ ¹⁷⁰
corrections. You can use a liquid that covers the

¹⁷⁵ ¹⁸⁰
error or an opaquing film that covers the error when

¹⁸⁵
you type over it.

After practicing corrections and entering scores, read the exercise for content.

New Work: Making Corrections

The method you use will depend on the kind of typewriter you are using. Refer to the manual of your electric or electronic typewriter for special instructions when making corrections with these machines.

The following methods and devices are used.

Correction Fluid is available in a bottle with a small brush or in pen form. Spread a thin coating over unwanted letters; wait for it to dry; type over it. This liquid is sold under the names of "Liquid Paper," "Wite-Out," "Paper Blend." It comes in white and in colors to use on colored paper. This is especially useful for manual typewriters and those electric that do not have correcting devices.

Coated Paper or *Opaquing Film* is sold under the name of Ko-Rec-Type. It may be used instead of correction fluid. It is inserted in front of the platen, coating side down, to cover the incorrect letter. It is used as follows:

(a) Backspace to the incorrect letter.
(b) Insert the coated paper over the error.
(c) Strike the incorrect letter so that the coating covers it.
(d) Remove the coated paper.
(e) Type the correction.

Those electric machines that use a ribbon cartridge have a **correction cartridge** to cover errors. After removing the ribbon cartridge:

(a) Insert the correction cartridge.
(b) Backspace to the error.
(c) Type the error again to cover it with a film.
(d) Replace the ribbon cartridge.
(e) Type the correction.

Electronic and some electric machines have *correction ribbon* or *correction film* threaded parallel with the typing ribbon. The ribbon covers unwanted letters; the film lifts off unwanted letters.

When using an electronic typewriter, tap the *correction key* (usually below the right shift key) as soon as you feel you have struck the wrong key. The error will have disappeared. If there is more than one wrong letter, hold your finger on the correction key. The machine will backspace and remove further letters. The machine may be programmed to erase from ten letters up to two lines. If your error is five spaces back, backspace to the error and tap the correction key. You may space forward or backspace, and the memory of the machine will erase the appropriate letter or letters. Thus, if you typed "fir" instead of "for," backspace to "i" and tap the correction key. You will now have a blank where "i" was. Just type "o." Tap the *relocation key;* it spaces forward automatically ready to continue typing. However, if you use the RETURN key or carrier release, the memory is canceled.

To make a correction outside of the memory range:

(a) Backspace to error.
(b) Tap the manual correction key.
(c) Hold down the correction key (not the manual) and strike the incorrect key.
(d) Release the correction key.
(e) Strike the correct letter.

If there is more than one letter to be corrected, repeat (c), (d), and (e).

When the corrections are completed, tap the manual correction key to activate the correction key.

On electric machines with correction ribbon, it works very much like the correction cartridge—the error must be repeated to remove it.

Some electronic machines have a *display screen* that shows a line or two of typing before it is printed. If the corrections are made while the letters are displayed, only the correct material will be printed.

It is wise to read the manual of your machine. There may be some variations of the methods described.

Erasable Paper. Typing can easily be erased from erasable paper with an eraser. This type of paper is not recommended for permanent records, since changes can be made too easily. It is useful for manuscript typing from which Xeroxed copies are to be made.

If none of the above methods are available, you may have to resort to using an *eraser*. Use a typewriter eraser that is not too stiff. Clean it by rubbing it on white paper. Move the carriage to the extreme right or left to prevent grit from falling into the machine. Roll your paper up so that the error rests on the platen. Erase with a light, short, circular motion, blowing lightly to keep the grit away from the machine. Use many light strokes rather than a few heavy strokes so that the surface of the paper remains smooth.

Double spacing

New Work Tryout

After studying the method that best suits your machine, make the corrections as indicated. Copy the material with the errors.

```
To type accurately, concentratoin is necessary.
                    (Change oi to io.)

It is necessary to develop the skill of proodreading.
                    (Change d to f.)
For a correction to be acceptable, it must be inbisible.
                    (Change b to v.)
Try not to erase any leffers except those which are
errors.
                    (Change ff to tt.)

We expect four guests.
                    (Change four to five, changing
                    three letters.)
```

Crowding and Spreading

Our next step in making corrections is to learn how to insert a word which has an extra letter (called *crowding*) and how to insert a word which has one letter less (called *spreading*).

Crowding. If you wish to substitute a four-letter word in place of a three-letter word, the three-letter word must be deleted. To gain an extra space, you must arrange to leave only half a space on each side of the four-letter word.   How you **half-space** will depend on your machine.

Half-space method

Electric and *electronic*.   Examine your machine to see if it has a half-space key.   When the half-space key is depressed, the carrier moves half a space; when it is released, it moves another half space.

Manual.   The space bar on most manual machines works like a half-space key—the carrier moves a half space on depressing and a half space on releasing.

If your electric machine does not have a half-space key, read ahead to the backspace method.

With either method, you will have to look at your fingers.

New Work Tryout

Double spacing

Type this sentence: `Meet me at one o'clock.`
You wish to change the time to *four* o'clock.

   (a) Erase **one**.   (The word **erase** does not necessarily mean with an eraser.)
   (b) Backspace as if to type over the **t** of **at**, and space forward once so that you are now in the space after **t**.
   (c) Depress the half-space key or space bar, and while holding it down, type **f**.
   (d) Release the half-space key or space bar and depress it again.   While holding it down, strike **o**.
   (e) Release and depress; strike **u**.
   (f) Release and depress; strike **r**.
   NOTE: You typed only on the down beat.   Your sentence looks like this in three stages.

```
Meet me at one o'clock.
Meet me at     o'clock.
Meet me at four o'clock.
```

In a full page of typing, the correction will be hardly noticeable.

Backspace method.   Use this method if your electric machine does not have a half-space key.   Type the sentence above; you want to change **one** to **four**.

   (a) Erase **one**.
   (b) Backspace as if to type over the **t** of **at**, and space forward twice so that you are now in the space where **o** was typed.
   (c) Depress the backspacer slightly, half a space.   Holding the backspacer steady, type **f**.
   (d) Release the backspacer and space forward once.
   (e) Again half-backspace and type **o**.
   (f) Release the backspacer and space forward once.
   (g) Half-backspace and type **u**.
   (h) Release the backspacer and space forward once.
   (i) Half-backspace and type **r**.

Self-Testing Work: Crowding

Assume that the following sentences were in the middle of a page of typing and you need to change them. Follow the method you just learned for crowding. Type a sentence, erase, and correct. Your sentences should look like this:

```
Tell him to bring lunch.          Change him to them.
Tell them to bring lunch.

The pears are delicious.          Change pears to apples.
The apples are delicious.

We expect early payment.          Change early to prompt.
We expect prompt payment.

Next week prices will be higher.    Change week to month.
Next month prices will be higher.
```

Spreading. When you need to replace a word with a new word that is one letter shorter, 1½ spaces must be left on each side of the new word. We follow the same method as for crowding, except that we start typing the new word an extra space to the right.

Type this sentence: `We found the machine in good condition.` To change **found** to **find**, erase **found**.

Half-space method
- (a) Bring the carrier to the **e** of **We**. Space for **e** and space once after **e**.
- (b) Now half-space and proceed by typing the word on the half space as you did for crowding.

Backspace method
- (a) Space for **e** and two spaces after **e**.
- (b) Half-backspace for each letter in the word as you did for crowding.

Your sentence should look like this in the three stages:

```
We found the machine in good condition.
We        the machine in good condition.
We find the machine in good condition.
```

Self-Testing Work: Spreading

Type each sentence and make the change indicated by spreading. When completed, your sentence should look like the second one.

```
We invited them to the party.     Change them to her.
We invited her  to the party.

Your black dress is suitable.     Change black to blue.
Your  blue dress is suitable.
```

```
This plan worked well.        Change worked to works.
This plan works well.
```

```
The meeting is on the first Monday of the month.
                         Change first to last.
The meeting is on the  last Monday of the month.
```

Inserting a comma without erasing

If a comma must be inserted on a typed page, it can be done without erasing, by half-spacing or half-backspacing.

Type this sentence:

```
After his interview he was offered the job.
```

Half-space method

To insert a comma after **interview**, bring the printing point over the last letter, **w**. Half space and strike the **comma**.

Backspace method

Bring the printing point to the space following **w**. Then depress the backspacer a little more than half and strike the **comma**. This needs practice.

Your sentence should look like this:

```
After his interview, he was offered the job.
```

Choose the method that gives you the better result on your machine.

Self-Testing Work

Copy the sentences exactly. Then insert a comma where indicated.

```
If you decide to subscribe send us your check for $10.
```
   Insert a comma after **subscribe.**

```
When we receive the order we shall send you our check.
```
   Insert a comma after **order**.

```
Order the following:  pears peaches apples and oranges.
```
   Insert commas after **pears** and **peaches**.

```
We decided therefore to close the office early.
```
   Insert commas after **decided** and **therefore**.

Challenge Work   *Double spacing*

On a full sheet, start 10 lines from the top edge of the paper and type the article on PROOFREADING so that it is perfect when you take the paper out of the machine. Make a correction the moment you are conscious of the error. Also proofread carefully, looking for errors, while the paper is still in the machine. It is best not to make any errors, but if you do, correct them so that they are not visible.

Study the page after you type it.

PROOFREADING

Every page of typing must be proofread carefully and corrected so that not a single error remains on the page. A good speller will spot typographical errors easily. A poor speller will not see errors as readily. But even a good speller who has been "speed reading" may not catch errors by just reading. Every word and particularly every number must be checked.

When proofreading, think of the meaning as well as the spelling. Watch for words that may be spelled correctly but that have different meanings like "stationery" and "stationary" or "break" and "brake" or "cite," "site," and "sight."

When proofreading a page, especially one that has numbers or symbols, it is best for one person to read from the original copy and a second person to check the typewritten copy <u>while it is still in the machine</u>. Punctuation marks should be read; paragraphing should be read.

If a person is not available for reading, use the forefinger of each hand to point along each line of both copies, glancing from one copy to the other, phrase by phrase, number by number. Be careful not to skip lines.

Proofreading is a skill that must be developed. Even a single uncorrected typing error will spoil the entire work.

LESSON 26

New Work: How to Type Personal Letters
Skill Building: Timings

15 (25)

72 (82)

Single spacing

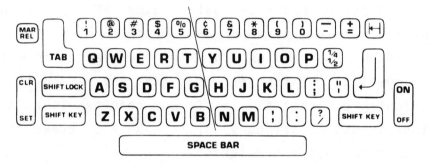

Warm-up: Say the drills as you type them.   Type each sentence five times.

    abcdefghijklmnopqrstuvwxyz abcdefghijklmnopqrstuvwxyz
    ala a!a s2s s@s d3d d#d f4f f$f f5f f%f j6j j¢j j7j j&j
    k8k k*k 191 l(l ;0; ;); ;-; ;_; ;=; ;+; ;½; ;¼; ;'; ;";

    The quick brown fox jumped over the lazy dogs.

    Now is the time for all good men to come to the aid of
    the party.

Skill-Building Work: The Parts of a Letter

1. Preview Practice—three times each

    personal   business   salutation   complimentary
    letterhead   stationery   described   consists
    extra   duplicate   post office   two-letter
    abbreviation   following   zip   capital   initials

Double Spacing

REMINDER: Make no corrections during timings.

2. Two One-Minute Timings

                                        5   10
        A personal letter consists of the following parts:

126

$$\overset{15}{} \qquad\qquad \overset{20}{}$$

the return address, the date, the salutation, the body

$$\overset{25}{} \qquad\qquad \overset{30}{}$$

of the letter and the complimentary close.

Center the title   THE PARTS OF A LETTER

3. Two Five-Minute Timings

$$\overset{5}{} \qquad\qquad \overset{10}{}$$

A personal letter consists of the following parts:

$$\overset{15}{} \qquad\qquad \overset{20}{}$$

the return address, the date, the salutation, the body

$$\overset{25}{} \qquad\qquad \overset{30}{}$$

of the letter and the complimentary close.

$$\overset{35}{} \qquad\qquad \overset{40}{}$$

In addition to the above, a business letter, which

$$\overset{45}{} \qquad\qquad \overset{50}{}$$

is typed on letterhead stationery that includes the

$$\overset{55}{} \qquad\qquad \overset{60}{}$$

return address, has two extra parts which are described

$$\overset{65}{}$$

below.

$$\overset{70}{} \qquad\qquad \overset{75}{}$$

The inside address follows the date, above the

$$\overset{80}{} \qquad\qquad \overset{85}{}$$

salutation. It consists of the full name and address

$$\overset{90}{} \qquad\qquad \overset{95}{}$$

of the person or firm to whom the letter is addressed.

$$\overset{100}{} \qquad\qquad \overset{105}{}$$

This is the same name and address which will be typed

$$\overset{110}{} \qquad\qquad \overset{115}{} \qquad\qquad \overset{120}{}$$

on the envelope. Use the two-letter post office ab-

$$\overset{125}{} \qquad\qquad \overset{130}{}$$

breviation for the state. Space twice before the zip.

$$\overset{135}{} \qquad\qquad \overset{140}{}$$

The full closing of a business letter, following

$$\overset{145}{} \qquad\qquad \overset{150}{}$$

the complimentary close, can consist of any or all of

$$\overset{155}{} \qquad\qquad \overset{160}{}$$

the following: the name of the firm, the name of the

$$\overset{165}{} \qquad\qquad \overset{170}{}$$

dictator, the title of the dictator. The initials of

$$\overset{175}{} \qquad\qquad \overset{180}{}$$

the dictator followed by a colon and the initials of

$$\overset{185}{} \qquad\qquad \overset{190}{}$$

the typist complete the closing.

$$\overset{195}{} \qquad\qquad \overset{200}{}$$

If a letter contains an enclosure, Enc. is typed

$$\overset{204}{}$$

under the initials.

After recording your scores, read the previous exercise for content.

New Work: Personal Letters
Make a copy of Model Letter 1 on a full sheet, 8½ × 11.
Margins 20 (30) and 65 (75). Tab stops at 25(35) and 42(50)   *Single spacing*
Set an additional tab after pivoting for the return address.

   If your stationery has your address printed on it, start typing with the date.   Otherwise, start with your two-line address followed by the date.   The three lines are single-spaced, all starting at the same point.

   Read the instructions under Model Letter 2 before typing this letter.
Model Letter 1
Personal letter
Semi-block form

          20   (30)   65   (75)

                                             725 Freedom Drive   18 lines
                                             Freeport, NY 11520
                                             February 15, 19--

         Dear Jane,   4

              I have just returned from a most exciting   2
         trip to Kenya. I spent ten days in the
         Reserves, observing animals in their home
         environment. Roles were reversed. We usually
         see animals in cages in a zoo. This time the
         animals saw us in our cages, the Safari cars
         in which we rode.

              I learned that outside of the dog and cat   2
         families such as lions, tigers, leopards and
         jackals, wild animals are vegetarians. Even
         the huge elephants live peacefully in the same
         area with giraffes and gazelles. And the meat-
         eating animals kill only when they are hungry.
         All the animals are protective parents.

              There goes the telephone. I'll write   2
         more next week.
                             42 (50)   2
                             Affectionately,

                                             (112 words)
Proofread and make corrections before removing the letter.

Model Letter 2
Personal letter
Semi-block form

18 lines

```
                          725 Freedom Drive
                          Freeport, NY  11520
                          February 21, 19--
```

```
Dear Jane,                                        4

     I am glad to receive your letter.  Yes, I
am sure you would enjoy a safari.  Since you
are a bird watcher, you will be thrilled with
the birds as well as the animals of Africa.

     There is a profusion of birds of every       2
size and variety you can imagine and some which
you can't imagine.  Even our ordinary starling
has iridescent feathers of brilliant blue in
Africa.

     The most voracious of the birds I saw is     2
the marabou stork.  The vultures line up and
wait until the marabou finishes eating before
they approach a carcass.

     I'll be glad to give you some travel tips     2
if you wish.

                    Affectionately,                2
```

(Between 100 and 125 words)

To determine where to set the tab stop for the return address and date, pivot from the right margin (backspace for each letter) for the widest line of the three lines. Set the tab stop.

The numbers on the right of the Model Letter indicate the number of lines down. (The number 4 means that you write on the fourth line.)

Copy Model 2. Note that for semi-block form, we block the return address and date, but we indent for paragraphs. Use the same line spacing as in Model 1. You have already set a tab stop for the return address for Letter Model 1. Use it. Make corrections.

Using the same margins and form as the Model letters, set up this letter. Substitute your own return address and today's date. Clear and reset the tab stop for your return address. Try to keep a fairly even right margin. The symbol (P) indicates where you should start a new paragraph.

Dear Jane: You seem to be worried about accommodations on the Reserves and in Nairobi. You will be amazed at how luxurious they are and what wonderful food is served. Be sure that your itinerary includes the Mount Kenya Safari Club. (P) It is good to be cautious and drink only bottled water anywhere in Kenya—even for brushing teeth. Talk to your doctor about antimalarial pills. Be prepared for washboard roads; however, the drivers are experts at changing flat tires. (P) Even though Kenya is on the Equator, it is about 7,000 feet above sea level and nights can be cool. The only season to avoid is the rainy season. Ask your travel agent.

Cordially,   (112 words)

If you are not completely satisfied with any of the three letters, type it again.

Margins for Personal Letters

You should now be able to set up and type your personal letters. Unless your letter is very short or very long, your margins should be 20 (30) and 65 (75). (For letters under 60 words, add 5 to the left margin and subtract 5 from the right margin. For letters over 175 words, subtract 5 from the left margin and add 5 to the right margin.)

The letters you have typed are between 100–125 words in length. You started typing eighteen lines down from the top edge for the address. If your stationery has a printed address, space nineteen lines down to the date for letters of this length.

If your letter falls in the 75–99 word group, add one line to the lines down; if it is in the 126–150 word group, subtract a line. In other words, make an adjustment of one line for each 25 words. A shorter letter needs a wider margin at the top; a longer letter needs a narrower margin.

After a short time at setting up letters, you will be able to approximate the number of words in the body of a letter at a glance.

Before you reach that point, do not count every word in the body of a letter. Instead, count the number of words in three successive lines; divide by three for the average; multiply this number by the lines in the body of the letter. This is a fair count of the words in the letter.

Challenge Work: Type a letter to a friend. It should be well placed on the page. The right margin should be fairly even. There should be no errors. The letter should be attractive and you should be pleased to send it.

LESSON 27

New Work: How to Type Business Letters
Skill-Building: Timings

15 (25)

72 (82)
Single spacing

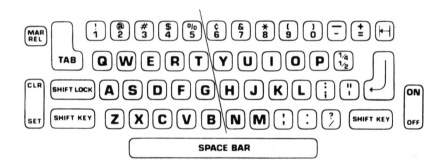

Warm-up: Say the drills as you type them.   Type the sentence five times.

```
aqaza swsxs dedcd frftfgfbfvf jujyjhjnjmj kik,k lol.l
;p;/;
al!a s2@s d3#d f4$f f5%f j6¢j j7&j k8*k l9(l ;0); ;-_;
;=+;
```

```
Now is the time for all good men to come to the aid of
the party.
```

Skill-Building Work: Styles of Business Letters

1. Preview Practice—three times each

```
styles      frequently      block      semi-block
principal      difference      paragraphs      similarly
indentations      companies      attractively      picture
resembles
```

Double spacing

2. Two One-Minute Timings

5   10

The two styles used most frequently for business

15   20

letters are the block and semi-block forms. The

25   30

principal difference between these two styles is that

35   40

paragraphs are not indented in the block form and are

45   48

indented in the semi-block form.

Center the heading   STYLES OF BUSINESS LETTERS

3. Two Five-Minute Timings

5   10

The two styles used most frequently for business

15   20

letters are the block and semi-block forms. The

25   30

principal difference between these two styles is that

35   40

paragraphs are not indented in the block form and are

45

indented in the semi-block form.

50   55

A number of companies prefer a strict block form

60   65

in typing letters. This form saves time since every

70   75

line, beginning with the date, starts at the left

80   85

margin. It is rather severe.

90   95

All letters should be attractively set up so that

100   105

a letter on a page resembles a picture in a frame. If

110   115

there is a difference between the top and bottom margins,

```
            120                              125
the bottom margin should be the wider one.  If there is
        130                      135
a difference between the left and right margins, the
 140                      145           147
left margin should be the wider one.
```

After practicing corrections and entering scores, read this again for content.

New Work: Parts of a Business Letter

Refer to Model Letter 3 as you read each paragraph.

A business letter is typed on **letterhead** stationery. The name, address, and telephone number of the firm are printed.

The **date** is the first item typed. Pivot for the date from the right margin. Set a tab stop. This tab stop will serve for all letters with the same margins until the end of the month. Make a note of the number of the tab.

The **inside address**, the name and address of the person or the firm to whom the letter is being sent, is blocked at the left margin in single spacing. (RETURN four times from the date to the inside address.)

The **salutation** followed by a colon (Dear Sir: Dear Madam: Gentlemen: Dear Mr. Jones: Dear Ms. Smith: My dear Mrs. Brown:) is typed at the left margin. (RETURN twice from the inside address to the salutation.)

The **body of the letter** in single spacing follows. (RETURN twice from the salutation to the body and twice between paragraphs.)

The **complimentary close** (Yours truly, Very truly yours, Sincerely, etc.) is typed at 42 (50). (RETURN twice between the body of the letter and the complimentary close.)

RETURN twice to the **full closing** at 42 (50) which may consist of the name of the firm in all caps; RETURN four times to the typewritten name of the dictator; RETURN once to the title of the dictator—any or all of these parts. The reason for the three blank lines above the dictator's typed name is to leave room for the handwritten signature of the dictator.

The initials of the dictator, a colon, and the initials of the typist—no spaces between—are typed at the left margin on the last line of the full closing.

If an **enclosure** is placed in the envelope with a letter, *Enc.* is typed a single space below the initials.

NOTE: The line spacing is easy to memorize.
(1) Within a part, use single spacing.
(2) There are only two places where you RETURN **four** times.
   a) after the date
   b) where the handwritten signature must appear
(3) RETURN twice between all other parts and between paragraphs.

Type an exact copy of Model Letter 3, block form. Correct all errors. Note: Tab at 42 (50). Set a tab for the date.

Type an exact copy of Model Letter 4, block form.

Model Letter 3
Block form
Full closing

CENTRAL REALTY COMPANY
349 Central Avenue
Fort Lee, New Jersey 07024

20 (30)   65 (75)

                                                                18

                                        March 10, 19—

                                                                4

Mr. Alexander Stern
210 Park Street
Fort Lee, NJ 07024

                                                                2

Dear Mr. Stern:

                                                                2

Our real estate company is looking for a house
for a client. He would like one near the park
on Park Street or on Seneca Street. He needs
a house with at least three bedrooms and two
bathrooms. It must have a garden.

Is your house for sale? If it is, please
write or telephone us. If it is not, do you
know of any house for sale in your neighbor-
hood?

                                                                2

Of course, we would have to inspect the house
at your convenience.

                                                                2

                    Yours very truly

                    CENTRAL REALTY COMPANY   2

                                                                4

                    Elliot R. Dunne
ERD:TS   President

                    (83 words)

Model Letter 4
Block form
Closing without a firm name or title

210 Park Street
Fort Lee, NJ   07024

17

March 12, 19--

4

Mr. Elliot R. Dunne
President, Central Realty Company
349 Central Avenue
Fort Lee, NJ   07024

2

Dear Mr. Dunne:

2

In answer to your letter of March 10, I am
interested in selling my house if I can get
a good price for it. It has not been offered
for sale in the past.

2

My house has five bedrooms, three on the second
floor and two on the third floor. The third
floor can be closed off. There are three bathrooms, one on each floor. I have just put in
a new heating system and I have recently re-
modeled the kitchen.

2

The best time for you to inspect the house is
between 10 a.m. and noon. Please telephone me
at my office 621-4587 and let me know what day
you will call.

2

Yours truly,

4

AS:FM   Alexander Stern

(113 words)

Letter Scale for Business Letters

No. of Words in Body	Margins		Lines to Date
60–140	20 (30)	65 (75)	18–16
141–240	15 (25)	70 (80)	16–14
241–300	10 (20)	75 (85)	14–12

Over 300, use two pages.

How to Use the Letter Scale.

If your letter is close to 60 words (in the 60's, 70's, or 80's), line space 18 to the date. If the letter is in the 90's, 100's, or 110's, line space 17. If the letter is in the 120's up to 140, line space 16. The longer the letter, the fewer lines down. Use the same principle for longer letters.

If a letter has fewer than 60 words, type the body of the letter in double spacing. Double the number of words to determine the margins and lines down. A letter of 50 words would count as 100. The inside address should still be typed in single spacing.

The average letter has three paragraphs. For each paragraph over three, subtract a line from the lines down to the date.

Notice in the above scale that the longer the letter, the narrower the margins.

To determine the number of words in the body of a letter, follow the same procedure as for personal letters:

 (a) count the number of words in three full lines
 (b) divide by three
 (c) multiply by number of lines.

Type a copy of Model Letter 5 in **semi-block** form. Set tabs for paragraphs and at the center, 42 (50).

I counted 24 words in 3 lines. There are 8 to a line. Multiplied by 17 lines, there are 136 words in this letter. Margins should be 20 (30) and 65 (75); 16 lines to date. However, the average letter has three paragraphs and this letter has four. For each paragraph over three, subtract one line. Therefore, come down 15 lines to the date.

Type a copy of Model Letter 6 in semi-block form.

The **subject line** is **centered,** two lines down from the salutation. Again, come down two lines to the body of the letter. Because of the two extra lines used when there is a subject line, **subtract** one line from the lines to the date.

This letter has 91 words. According to the scale, the lines to the date should be 17. Subtract one line for the subject line. Come down 16 lines from the top edge.

Model Letter 5
Semi-block

October 15, 19--

Elite Furniture Company
P.O. Box 19891
High Point, NC   27262

Gentlemen:

On September 24 we ordered a #36 mahogany
table and 12 matching chairs for our conference
room. They were delivered this morning.

On unpacking, we find that the chairs you
sent are walnut, not mahogany. We ordered the
seats and backs in burgundy leather; the chairs
you sent have seats and backs of gold cloth.

We can repack the chairs. However, you
should be responsible for their return. It
might be best if your truck picked them up
when you deliver the mahogany chairs. We shall
have to store them in the basement meanwhile.

Obviously, we are disappointed. Please
let us know by return mail when you will make
delivery. We have scheduled several confer-
ences for the last week in October and the
first week in November; we need the chairs.

Yours truly,

Richard S. Fine
Office Manager

RSF:REW

Model Letter 6
Semi-block with subject line

                                        Type today's date

          Bradford & Curtis, Inc.
          1200 Western Avenue
          Los Angeles, CA 90015

          Gentlemen:
               Subject: Care of Your Air Conditioners

               Two years ago you bought five air condi-
          tioners for your office. Your warranty ex-
          pired this month. The air conditioners should
          be inspected for wear, cleaned and adjusted
          before the summer season.

               You could sign up for a service contract
          which would cover all service calls and parts
          for the next year, or you could pay for indi-
          vidual service calls and for parts.

               Compare the prices listed on the enclosed
          brochure. Let us know which plan suits you.
          The work should be done now, before the heat
          sets in.

                                   Yours very truly

                                   AIR CONTROL COMPANY

          SDF:OP   Saul D. Frank
          Enc.   Supervisor

                         (91 words)

Type a copy of Model Letter 7 in semi-block form.

The **attention** line is centered two lines down from the inside address. Because this 47-word letter is under 60 words, we type it in double spacing and set it up like a letter of 94 words.

REMEMBER: The **attention** line is under the **inside address**. The **subject** line is under the **salutation**.

Model Letter 7
Semi-block with Attention line
Double spacing—short letter

                                        Type today's date

                                                              4

          Air Control Company
          1405 Atlantic Avenue
          Los Angeles, CA   90015

                    Attention of Mr. Saul D. Frank

          Gentlemen:

               I am enclosing a check for $185 to cover

          the contract for service and parts on our five

          air conditioners for one year. Please send us

          the policy.

               We shall expect your service man within

          the next ten days. Let us know in advance

          when he will call.

                              Yours truly,

                              BRADFORD & CURTIS, INC.

                                                              4

          ECC:TR   Edward C. Curtis
          Enc.

                         (47 words)

LESSON 28

New Work: How to Type Envelopes
                How to Fold Letters for Insertion
Skill-Building: Timings

15 (25)

70 (80)
Single spacing

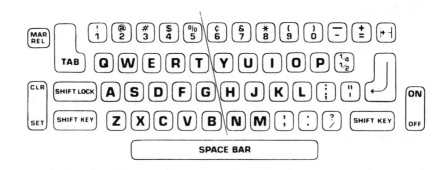

Warm-up:

1. Say the drills as you type them.

   ```
   ala a!a s2s s@s d3d d#d f4f f$f f5f f%f j6j j¢j j7j j&j
   k8k k*k 191 1(1 ;0; ;); ;-; ;_; ;=; ;+; ;½; ;¼; ;'; ;";
   ```

2. Close your eyes and type the alphabet twice.
3. With eyes closed, type numbers from 1 through 100.
4. Practice corrections.
5. For review of @ # $ % ¢

   ```
   85 #621 @ $95.57; 22 #68 @ 26¢; 50 #39 @ 75¢; 4 #7 @ 5¢
   15% of $85; 12% of $47; 17% of $3,789; 9.3% of $45,000
   ```

6. Type this sentence five times.

```
Now is the time for all good men to come to the aid of
the party.
```

Skill-Building Work: Typing Envelopes

1. Preview Practice—three times each.

```
when      presented    dictator    signature    zip
envelope     properly     accompany     accuracy
blocked     designated     capital     blank     usually
upper     corner
```

Double spacing

2. Two One-Minute Timings

```
                        5                        10
     When a letter is presented to the dictator for his
                   15                    20
signature, a properly addressed envelope should accom-
             25
pany the letter.
                        30                        35
     The address on the envelope is the same as the in-
                 40
side address of the letter.
```

Center the title   TYPING ENVELOPES

Two Five-Minute Timings

$\overset{5}{\text{When a letter is presented to the dictator for his}}$ ... 10

```
                                   5                          10
     When a letter is presented to the dictator for his
              15                      20
signature, a properly addressed envelope should accom-
                 25
pany the letter.
                                30                       35
     The address on the envelope is the same as the in-
              40                       45
side address of the letter.  Always check the accuracy
              50                       55
of the address on both the letter and envelope.
                          60                       65
     The post office prefers that envelopes be typed in
              70                       75
all capital letters, single spacing, blocked, with the
              80                       85
state designated by two letters.  The zip code follows
              90                       95                    100
the state on the same line.  If the zip is omitted, de-
                          105
livery of the letter will be delayed.
                          110                         115
     The return address is usually printed in the upper
              120                      125
left corner of the envelope.  If you are using a blank
              130                      135
envelope, type the return address, blocked, two lines
140                          145                          150
down from the top edge of the upper left corner and two
                 152
spaces in.
```

After recording scores, read the exercise again for content.

New Work: Addressing Envelopes

The most widely used business envelopes are:
1. The commercial or **No. 6** envelope ($6\frac{1}{2}'' \times 3\frac{5}{8}''$).
2. The legal or No. **10** envelope ($9\frac{1}{2}'' \times 4\frac{1}{8}''$).

With the installing of high-speed Optical Character Readers (OCRs) in the post office, the U.S. Postal Service requests the placement of the address be typed for automatic reading.

The following instructions follow the guidelines. The envelope should be typed in all capital letters. *Nothing should be typed on the envelope below the line with the zip code.*

To Address a **No. 6** Envelope:
1. Insert envelope, flap edge first, left edge at 0 on the scale.
2. Set left margin at **25 (35)** on the scale.
3. Space **12** single lines from top edge of envelope.
4. Type address in all capital letters, block form, single spacing. Within the U.S. the last line consists of the town or city, the two-letter designation of the state, and the zip code. However, if the letter is sent to a foreign country, the name of the country should be typed on a separate last line.

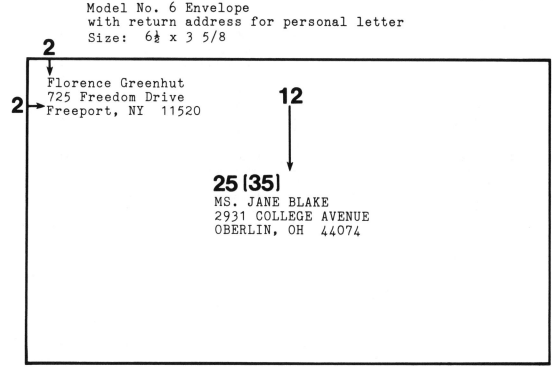

```
          Model No. 6 Envelope
          with return address for personal letter
          Size:  6½ x 3 5/8
```

Make a copy of the above No. 6 envelope.

Fig. 45 No. 6 envelope

To Address a **No. 10** Envelope (Fig. 46)
1. Insert envelope, flap edge first, left edge at 0.
2. Set left margin at **42 (50)**.
3. Space **14** single lines from top edge of envelope.
4. Type address in all capital letters, block form, single spacing.

TWO-LETTER STATE NAME ABBREVIATIONS

Alabama	AL	Montana	MT	
Alaska	AK	Nebraska	NE	
Arizona	AZ	Nevada	NV	
Arkansas	AR	New Hampshire	NH	
American Samoa	AS	New Jersey	NJ	
California	CA	New Mexico	NM	
Canal Zone	CZ	New York	NY	
Colorado	CO	North Carolina	NC	
Connecticut	CT	North Dakota	ND	
Delaware	DE	Ohio	OH	
District of Columbia	DC	Oklahoma	OK	
Florida	FL	Oregon	OR	
Georgia	GA	Pennsylvania	PA	
Guam	GU	Puerto Rico	PR	
Hawaii	HI	Rhode Island	RI	
Idaho	ID	South Carolina	SC	
Illinois	IL	South Dakota	SD	
Indiana	IN	Tennessee	TN	
Iowa	IA	Trust Territories	TT	
Kansas	KS	Texas	TX	
Kentucky	KY	Utah	UT	
Louisiana	LA	Vermont	VT	
Maine	ME	Virginia	VA	
Maryland	MD	Virgin Islands	VI	
Massachusetts	MA	Washington	WA	
Michigan	MI	West Virginia	WV	
Minnesota	MN	Wisconsin	WI	
Mississippi	MS	Wyoming	WY	
Missouri	MO			

If there is an **attention** line or any other special instruction, such as **hold, forward, department number**, type it on a separate line under the name of the addressee.

Now, address a No. 6 and a No. 10 envelope for each of the business letters in Lesson 27.

(Printed return address)

14 →

42[50]
AIR CONTROL COMPANY
ATTENTION: MR. SAUL D. FRANK
1405 ATLANTIC AVENUE
LOS ANGELES, CA 90015

Model No. 10 Envelope
with Attention line

Size: 9½ x 4 1/8

Fig. 46 No. 10 envelope

Fig. 47 For No. 6 Envelope (6½″ by 3⅝″)

1. Fold from the bottom to within about ⅛ inch of the top edge.

2. Fold from right to left a little less than ⅓ of the width.

3. Fold again from left to right, leaving about ⅛ inch margin.

4. Insert the folded letter in the envelope:
   (a) Hold the envelope with the reverse side facing you.
   (b) Insert folded letter with open end at top.

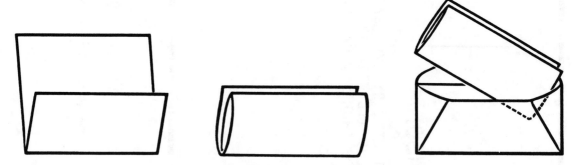

Fig. 48 For No. 10 Envelope (9½″ by 4⅛″)

1. Fold from the bottom to a little less than ⅓ of the sheet.

2. Fold again to within about ⅛ of an inch from the top edge.

3. Insert the folded letter into the envelope:
   (a) Hold the envelope with the reverse side facing you.
   (b) Insert the letter with the open end at the top.

FOLDING LETTERS

Following the instructions above, fold all the letters you typed in Lesson 27 for No. 6 and No. 10 envelopes. You have twice as many envelopes as letters, so fold blank papers for the additional envelopes.

Insert the letters in the envelopes.

LESSON 29

New Work: How to Make Carbon Copies
How to Make Corrections on Carbon Copies
Skill-Building: Timings

15 (25)

72 (82)
Single spacing

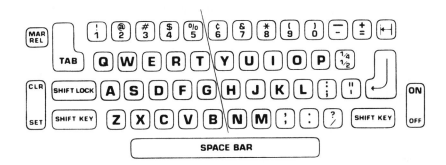

Warm-up:

1. Say the drills as you type them.

```
aqaza swsxs dedcd frftfgfbfvf jujyjhjnjmj kik,k lol.l
;p;/; ala a!a s2s s@s d3d d#d f4f f$f f5f f%f j6j j¢j
j7j j&j k8k k*k 191 1(1 ;0; ;); ;-; ;_; ;=; ;+; ;½;
;¼; ;'; ;"; ;/; ;?;
```

2. Type the sentence five times.

```
The quick brown fox jumped over the lazy dogs.
```

3. Review of ! & * ( ). Type twice.

```
Today! Pratt & Brixton are reducing every item.
Doors open early!*  (At both store and warehouse.)

*At 8:30 a.m.

Regal & Jones require a deposit of forty dollars ($40).
Coe & Ericson* insist on a fee of ninety dollars ($90).

*Lawyers
```

Skill-Building Work: Carbon Copies

Preview Practice—three times each.

```
piece      correspondence    office    facsimile      wipe
although    know     carbon copies    corrections
smudges    high-grade      touching    original
```

Double spacing

Two One-Minute Timings

```
                             5                       10
        Every piece of correspondence that leaves an office
                      15                      20
should have a facsimile in the file.  Although most busi-
            25                      30
ness offices have copying machines, some do not; nor do
       35                      40
homes.  Therefore, it is necessary to know how to make
     45                      50          53
carbon copies of correspondence and reports.
```

Center the title CARBON COPIES

Two Five-Minute Timings

Every piece of correspondence that leaves an office
should have a facsimile in the file. Although most business offices have copying machines, some do not; nor do
homes. Therefore, it is necessary to know how to make
carbon copies of correspondence and reports.

The carbon copies should be an exact duplicate of
the original. If a change is made on the original, it
must be made on the carbon copy or copies. If an error
is corrected on the original, it must be corrected on
the carbon copy or copies. Corrections should be as neat
as on the original. There should be no smudges on the
carbon copies.

Use a high-grade carbon paper to avoid smudges. If
a carbon paper is creased, discard it. If any carbon
dirties your hand, be sure to wipe it clean before touching any of the papers.

In this lesson you will learn how to make carbon
copies and how to make corrections on carbon copies.

After practicing corrections and entering your scores, read this exercise again for content.

New Work: How to Make Carbon Copies

For the copy, do not use letterhead paper, which is expensive. If the copy is for the file, your office may use paper which has "Copy" imprinted on it. Whether or not you should use bond paper depends on the use of the copy. In most cases, copies are typed on a cheaper grade of paper.

You might use a **carbon set** in which the carbon paper is attached to the copy paper.

To type an original and a carbon copy:
1. With the shiny side of the carbon paper away from you, cut or tear off a small triangle at the upper left-hand corner.
2. Place the **copy** paper flat on your desk, **right side up.**
3. Place the **carbon, shiny** side **down,** on the copy paper.
4. Place the **letterhead paper, right** side **up,** on the carbon paper.
5. With the top and left sides even, insert the three papers in the machine. (The shiny side of the carbon will face you as you are ready to place it behind the platen.)
6. If necessary, straighten the papers.
7. With the first word you type, check to see that the impression on the copy is correct. If not, remove the papers and start again.

If you should need three carbon copies, the papers are stacked as follows:
1. **Copy** paper face **up.**
2. **Carbon** face **down.**
3. **Copy** paper face **up.**
4. **Carbon** face **down.**
5. **Copy** paper face **up.**
6. **Carbon** paper face **down.**
7. **Letterhead** paper face **up.**

If you need 4 or 5 or 6 carbons, stack the extra copy papers and carbons in the same manner before placing the original on top.

Some machines have a pressure adjustment for heavier typing for multiple carbons, numbered 1 to 10.

To insert multiple carbons evenly:
1. Place the stack of papers between the flap and back of an envelope.
2. Roll the pack through the platen until the envelope is free.
3. Remove the envelope.
4. Roll back until the papers are in typing position.

If the stack is too thick, use the paper release to enable you to roll the pack into place. Position the papers and lock the paper release.

When inserting a carbon pack, be sure to insert the open end. Otherwise, no corrections can be made on the copy.

After the page is complete (typed, proofread, corrected), remove the papers with your left hand as you work the paper release with your right hand. Then take hold of all the papers in the upper left-hand corner between your thumb and forefinger, shake the papers, and the carbon papers (which have the left corners cut away) will fall out. This prevents smudging.

To apply what you have learned, insert papers for an original and a carbon copy of the following letter. Use today's date. Type it in semi-block form with appropriate margins and placement.

REMINDER: After the first word of the date, check the carbon copy to see if the word appears there.

This letter has 68 words. Use your initials as the typist's.

Mrs. Agnes Folger
2532 Beekman Place
Elkhart, IN 46514

Dear Mrs. Folger:

With a dinner on Monday, April 17, at 8 p.m. we are launching our annual drive to fund research for Disabled Children.

During the past twelve months, our research has resulted in an important breakthrough. The featured speaker, Dr. Aaron Ellison, will tell us about the dramatic results. Disabled Children are already benefiting from it.

Tickets for the dinner are $50, tax deductible. Please make your reservation soon. Sincerely, Peter J. Smith, Chairman   PJS:—

How to Make Corrections on Carbon Copies
  1. **Ko-Rec-Type Method**
     Ko-Rec-Type makes an opaquing film especially for carbon copies. It works well for any method of correction which corrects errors by typing over them on the original (correction film, correction ribbon, Ko-Rec-Type). As the error is lifted off or covered on the original, the error is covered on the carbon copy.
     (a) Roll the platen two lines below the error.
     (b) Lift the paper bail.
     (c) Place the correction film, dull side down, between the carbon paper and the carbon copy, covering the error.
     (d) Roll back to the error on the original.
     (e) Using the manual correction key or the correction cartridge or Ko-Rec-Type, type the error again.
     (f) Remove the carbon Ko-Rec-Type.
     (g) Lower the paper bail and type the correction on the original.

2. **Liquid Correction Method**
Cover the error on the original and on the carbon copy, being sure that both are completely dry before permitting the carbon paper to touch the copy.   Then type the correction.

3. **Eraser Method**
    (a) Roll the platen two lines below the error.
    (b) Lift the paper bail.
    (c) Place an index card (or $\frac{1}{4}$ of an index card) between the carbon paper and the carbon copy, covering the error.
    (d) Erase the error on the original by any method.
    (e) Use a pencil eraser to erase the error on the carbon copy, protecting your fingers from the carbon paper with the index card.
    (f) Remove the index card.
    (g) Lower the paper bail and type the correction on the original.

If you have more than one carbon copy, put card insertions in front of each carbon copy.   Start all corrections with the original and work back.

REMINDER: Remove all insertions before typing on the original.   Otherwise, you will have a blank on the carbon copies.

Type the following exercise with two carbon copies.   Aim at perfect work, but if you should make an error, correct it on the original and the carbon copies.   Follow the instructions for the method you choose, step by step.

CORRECTIONS ON CARBON COPIES

After reading all of the instructions about correcting errors on originals and carbon copies, it is obvious
that it is much better to type accurately and avoid
errors. You could easily type a sentence or more in
the time it takes to correct an error on a carbon copy.

Never erase on the original without protecting the
carbon copy with a card. Without such protection, an
erasure on the original would result in a dark smudge
on the carbon copy. And any typing to lift off errors
would only darken those errors on the carbon copy.

The protecting card can serve another purpose.
If you wish to add a personal note on the original without having it appear on the carbon, insert a card to
cover the area on the copy.

It is important to remove the card or cards as soon
as erasures are made and before the correction is typed.

Challenge Work: Type this paragraph with a carbon copy and pay attention to the
content.

If you should decide to make a change or a correction after an original and carbon copy are removed from
the machine, delete the unwanted letters with liquid or
eraser on each paper. Separate the papers. Do not try
to reinsert the papers with the carbon. Reinsert the
carbon copy first. Align it carefully before typing
the correction. If your machine has a ribbon setting
for disengaging the ribbon (such as a setting for cutting
stencils), disengage the ribbon so that the impression
of the key you strike is very light and can be easily
erased if it is too high or too low. After proper alignment, type the correction. Do the same with the
original.

LESSON 30

New Work: Setting Up a Tabulation
Skill-Building: Timings

15 (25)

72 (82)
Single spacing

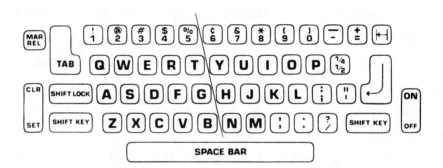

Warm-up:

1. Close your eyes and type the alphabet two times.
2. With eyes closed, type numbers from 1 to 100.
3. Practice on $-$ _ $=$ $+$ $\frac{1}{2}$ $\frac{1}{4}$ ' " / ?

```
;-; ;_; ;=; ;+; ;½; ;¼; ;'; ;"; ;/; ;?;
36½ x 9 = 328½.  38 ÷ 8 = 4 3/4.  79½ + 28¼ = 107 3/4.
8½ + 3¼ = 11 3/4.  27¼ + 16½ = 43 3/4.  59½ - 7¼ = 52¼.
```

        Are you traveling first class? <u>First-class</u> plane
tickets cost more than <u>economy-class</u> tickets. A <u>first-</u>
<u>class</u> ticket provides more leg room, a wider seat,
liquor, an elaborate meal, attentive service, and a
larger luggage allowance.

Skill-Building: Tabulation

    1. Preview Practice—three times each

```
tabulation    information    systematic    condensed
columns     presented    easy    equal    distance
horizontally    across    centered    sub-heading
```

Double Spacing

2. Two One-Minute Timings. If you finish before the minute is up, start again.

```
                        5                              10
    A tabulation presents information in a systematic
                  15                          20
and condensed form, arranged in columns.  Thus presented,
              25                      30
it should be easy to read and understand.
```

Center the heading   **TABULATION**

    3. Two Five-Minute Timings

```
                          5                                10
    A tabulation presents information in a systematic
                  15                          20
and condensed form, arranged in columns.  Thus presented,
              25                          30
it should be easy to read and understand.
                          35
    A tabulation should have equal left and right
  40                          45                      50
margins.  The top and bottom margins should be equal.
                  55
The distance between columns should be equal.
          60                          65                      70
    We set the left margin for the first column and set
              75
tab stops for every other column.
```

                            80   85
            Because information is usually presented horizon-
                      90   95
    tally, a tabulation should always be typed across the
                100
    page, line by line.
                                105   110
            The main heading is always centered, usually in
                        115   120
    all capital letters.   A subheading is also centered.
                      125   130
    If there are column headings, each one is centered over
              135
    its column.

After entering scores, read this exercise for content.

New Work: How to set up a tabulation.

Review of vertical centering for equal top and bottom margins.
 1. Count the lines in the tabulation (typed and blank).
 2. Subtract from 66, the lines on a 8½ × 11 sheet of paper.
 3. Divide by 2. The result is the number of lines from the top edge of the paper to the heading.

Two-Column Tabulation

Double spacing

```
COUNTRIES IN WESTERN EUROPE AND THEIR CAPITALS


            Austria          Vienna

            Belgium          Brussels

            Denmark          Copenhagen

            France           Paris

            Ireland (Eire)   Dublin

            Luxembourg       Luxembourg

            Netherlands      Amsterdam

            Norway           Oslo

            Spain            Madrid

            Sweden           Stockholm

            Switzerland      Bern

            United Kingdom   London

            West Germany     Bonn
```

To set up this two-column tabulation, follow this procedure, step by step:

1. Move margin stops to extreme left and right.

2. Clear tab stops except the one at the center, 42 (50).

3. Vertical placement
   (a) Count lines in tabulation—29.
   (b) $66 - 29 = 37$.
   (c) $37 \div 2 = 18\frac{1}{2}$. Drop $\frac{1}{2}$. 18 lines down from top edge.

4. Insert paper and come down 18 lines (9 double).

5. Center title and type in all caps.

6. RETURN twice (4 lines down)

7. To determine **left margin** stop:
   (a) On another sheet of paper, draw this diagram for the two columns and the spaces between. We shall leave six spaces between columns. (There is no rule about this number; you might like more or less.)

——————————————— 6 ———————————————

   (b) Count the number of spaces in the widest item in each column. United Kingdom = 14. Copenhagen = 10.

(c) Enter the numbers in the appropriate columns in your diagram.   It should now look like this:

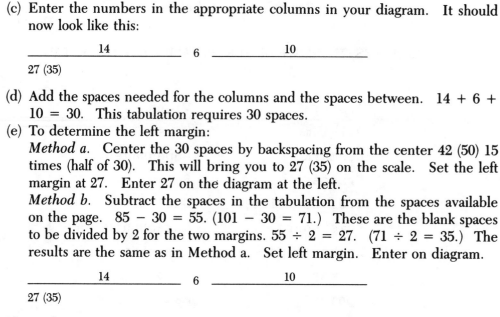

(d) Add the spaces needed for the columns and the spaces between.   14 + 6 + 10 = 30.   This tabulation requires 30 spaces.

(e) To determine the left margin:
Method a.   Center the 30 spaces by backspacing from the center 42 (50) 15 times (half of 30).   This will bring you to 27 (35) on the scale.   Set the left margin at 27.   Enter 27 on the diagram at the left.
Method b.   Subtract the spaces in the tabulation from the spaces available on the page.   85 − 30 = 55.   (101 − 30 = 71.)   These are the blank spaces to be divided by 2 for the two margins. 55 ÷ 2 = 27.   (71 ÷ 2 = 35.)   The results are the same as in Method a.   Set left margin.   Enter on diagram.

8. Clear tab stop at center.

9. To determine the tab stop for the second column:
From the left margin, space forward for the first column (14) plus the spaces between columns (6).   This will bring the carrier to 47 (55).   Set the tab stop. Enter on the diagram.   Your diagram should now look like this:

Of course, you need only one set of numbers—either for pica or elite.

10. Test your machine to see that your left margin is at 27 (35) and your tab is at 47 (55).   Check to see that you are two double line spaces below the heading.

11. Type the tabulation, starting with Austria, tab key, Vienna, RETURN, Belgium, tab key, Brussels, RETURN, etc.   Type across each line horizontally.

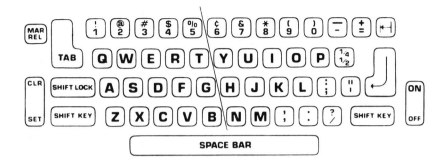

Set tab at 42 (50)

Set up and diagram the following tabulation. Note that the heading consists of two lines, double spaced. Leave two double line spaces between the heading and the body of the tabulation.

INDEPENDENT COUNTRIES IN SOUTH AMERICA

AND THEIR CAPITALS

Argentina	Buenos Aires
Bolivia	La Paz
Brazil	Brasilia
Chile	Santiago
Colombia	Bogota
Ecuador	Quito
Guyana	Georgetown
Paraguay	Asuncion
Peru	Lima
Uruguay	Montevideo
Venezuela	Caracas

Follow each step in turn that we listed in the first tabulation, substituting the new numbers.

Before typing the tabulation, compare your diagram with the following:

(19 lines down from top edge)

_____ 9 _____ 6 _____ 12 _____

29 (37)   44 (52)

Three-Column Tabulation

```
THE ORIGINAL THIRTEEN STATES
Area in Square Miles and Date of Admission


      Delaware          2,057    December 7, 1787

      Pennsylvania     45,333    December 12, 1787

      New Jersey        7,846    December 18, 1787

      Georgia          58,876    January 2, 1788

      Connecticut       5,009    January 9, 1788

      Massachusetts     8,257    February 6, 1788

      Maryland         10,577    April 28, 1788

      South Carolina   31,055    May 23, 1788

      New Hampshire     9,304    June 21, 1788

      Virginia         40,815    June 25, 1788

      New York         49,576    July 26, 1788

      North Carolina   52,712    November 21, 1789

      Rhode Island      1,214    May 29, 1790
```

To set up a 3-column tabulation, follow the same procedure as for 2-column tabulation.

1. Clear margins and tab stops except for the tab stop at the center.
2. Figure lines down for vertical placement. Note that the sub-heading is one double space below the main heading.
3. Center the headings. RETURN twice.
4. Make diagram of three columns and spaces between.
5. Count the widest item in each column.

————— 14 ————— 6 ————— 6 ————— 6 ————— 17 —————

6. Add the columns and spaces between. (49)
7. *Method a.* Center 49. (Backspace 24 from the center.) Left margin is 18 (26).
   Method b. Subtract 49 from 85 (101) and divide by 2. Left margin is 18 (26). Set the margin stop and enter on the diagram.
8. Clear tab stop at center.
9. From the left margin, space once for every letter in the widest item of the first column plus 6. Set the tab at 38 (46). Enter on the diagram.
10. From the tab stop for column 2, space for every letter in the widest item in column 2 plus 6. Set the tab at 50 (58). Enter on the diagram.

————— 14 ————— 6 ————— 6 ————— 6 ————— 17 —————

18 (26)   38 (46)   50 (58)

11. Test margin and tab stops against the numbers on the diagram. It is important that all numbers be entered on the diagram as you go along so that you have a record of your calculations.

Three-Column Tabulation with Short Headings

THE CITY OF NEW YORK

General Obligation Bonds

<u>Due</u>	<u>Amount</u>	<u>Rate</u>
1990	$11,230,000	8.60 %
1991	11,380,000	8 7/8
1992	9,745,000	9
1993	9,905,000	9¼
1994	5,075,000	9½
1995	5,305,000	9 5/8
1996	5,355,000	9 3/4
1997	6,120,000	9 7/8
1998	6,140,000	10
1999	6,140,000	10
2000	6,140,000	10

When figuring the widest item of each column in this tabulation, include the dollar sign in column 2. In column 3, count the widest spread in the column: the % sign should extend beyond 8 7/8; the line begins with 10 which you will find below. Therefore, the line is counted as if it were 10 7/8%, seven characters.

When typing **numbers** in columns, be sure that **units** are typed **under units.** When typing column 3, remember to space once for the figures in the first eight lines, until you get to 10 on the ninth line.

NOTE: $ and % signs are not repeated after the first line.

Calculate and diagram this tabulation; set margin and tab stops.

Column Headings: Each column heading is centered over the widest item in the column. To center a column heading that is narrower than the column:
1. From the beginning of the column (margin or tab stop), space forward once for every second letter of the widest item. This is the center of the column.
2. Backspace once for every second letter of the heading.
3. Type the heading.

Two-Column Tabulation with Headings

Figure the vertical placement for the following tabulation with proper line spacing after the heading. Center the main heading. Make the diagram. Center the headings over the columns. Type the tabulation.

EQUIVALENT AMERICAN AND BRITISH TERMS

United States	England
wrench	spanner
gasoline	petrol
hood (of a car)	bonnet
rest room	cloakroom
toilet	closet
closet	cupboard, wardrobe
line	queue
check	cheque
diaper	napkin
napkin	serviette
aluminum	aluminium
welfare	dole

Three-Column Tabulation with Wide Headings

TEN HIGHEST MOUNTAIN PEAKS IN THE UNITED STATES

Name of Peak	In the Mountain Range	Altitude in Feet
McKinley	Alaska Range	20,300
North Peak	" "	19,370
Foraker	" "	17,280
Blackburn	Wrangell Mountains	16,140
Whitney	Sierra Nevadas	14,495
Elbert	Rocky Mountains	14,431
Harvard	" "	14,420
Massive	" "	14,418
Rainier	Cascade Range	14,390
Blanca	Rocky Mountains	14,390

Since this is a wide tabulation, leave only 4 spaces between columns. (You may leave 3 if you wish.)

The **widest** item in each column is the **column heading**. Count the letters in the headings and enter in the diagram.

1. After centering the main heading, type the column headings.
2. Center the widest item in each column under its heading.
   (a) Space forward once for every second letter in the heading.
   (b) Backspace once for every second letter in the widest item. Reset the margin or tab stop.
3. Change the numbers in the diagram.
4. Check margin and tab stops. Be sure old ones are cleared.

Ditto Marks. Use quotation marks. Type in the center of the word above. To find the center, space forward once for every second letter, as you've done before.

Statistical Typing. Typists who do a great deal of statistical tabulations often prefer to remove their fingers from the guide keys and cover the keys 1, 2, 3, 4 with the left hand and the keys 7, 8, 9, 0 with the right hand.

LESSON 31

New Work: Use of Variable Line Spacer
Use of Ratchet Release in typing mathematical equations and chemical
formulas as well as in drawing vertical lines
Skill-Building: Timings
15 (25)   72 (82)

Single spacing

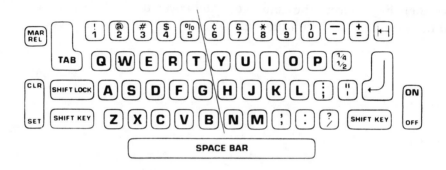

Warm-up: Type the drills once and each sentence five times.

```
aqaza swsxs dedcd frftfgfbfvf jujyjhjnjmj kik,k lol.l
;p;/; ala a!a s2s s@s d3d d#d f4f f$f f5f f%f j6j j¢j
j7j j&j k8k k*k 191 1(1 ;0; ;); ;-; ;_; ;=; ;+; ;½;
;¼; ;'; ;"; ;/; ;?;
```

The quick brown fox jumped over the lazy dogs.

Now is the time for all good men to come to the aid of
the party.

Practice on ' " ?   Type twice.

Are you going to the performance of "Hamlet" today?
Don't buy a ticket for me. I'll buy my own.

The picture measures 2' 7" by 3' 4".
Where? Why? How? How much? What does it cost?

Skill-Building Timings

Preview Practice—three times each

```
plane      reservations    long–distance    destination
example    California       continental      United States
Eastern    Central    Mountain    Pacific     time zones
hour's     Spring forward!     Fall back!
```

Double spacing

Two One-Minute Timings

```
                         5                         10
When making plane reservations and when making long–
              15                        20
distance telephone calls, it is essential to know the
              25                        30
local time of arrival at your destination and the local
        35                        40
time your telephone call is received.
```

Type the heading   TIME ZONES

Two Five-Minute Timings

After practicing corrections for the first timing, make a carbon copy of the second timing.

```
                         5                         10
When making plane reservations and when making long–
              15                        20
distance telephone calls, it is essential to know the
              25                        30
local time of arrival at your destination and the local
        35                        40
time your telephone call is received.
                         45                        50
As an example, if a person in California places a
              55                        60
call to an office in New York at 4 p.m. Pacific time,
              65                        70
the New York office would most likely be closed since it
```

75   80

would be 7 p.m. Eastern time in New York. On the other

85   90

hand, if a person in New York calls California at 10 a.m.

95   100

Eastern time, it would be 7 a.m. in California.

105   110

There are four time zones in continental United

115   120   125

States. There is an hour's difference in time between

130   135

zones. Starting on the East Coast, the latest in time,

140   145

the zones are: Eastern, Central, Mountain, Pacific. At

150   155

12 noon Eastern, it is 11 a.m. Central, 10 a.m. Mountain,

160

and 9 a.m. Pacific.

165   170

For half a year during the winter season, we have

175   180

Standard time. During the summer season, the clock is

185   190   195

put forward one hour and we have Daylight Saving Time in

all time zones.

200   205

To adjust the clock in April and October, remember:

210   215

Spring forward! Fall back!

Before removing the second timing from the machine, proofread and make corrections on the original and the copy.

New Work

Typing the Time. Following a figure, lowercase a.m. and uppercase A.M. are both correct. Similarly p.m. and P.M. are both correct provided a figure precedes. Be consistent when typing a letter or article. Type:

```
7 a.m., 7 A.M.; 8 a.m., 8 A.M.; 9 a.m., 9 A.M.; 10 a.m.
1 p.m., 1 P.M.; 2 p.m., 2 P.M.; 3 p.m., 3 P.M.; 4 p.m.
```

Two ways of typing on lines other than those fixed by the line-spacing mechanism.

Ratchet Release

This is a lever to be found near the left-hand roller knob. On some machines it is a setting on the line-space gauge marked "R." The ratchet release makes it possible to write above or below the writing line (as in algebraic terms and chemical formulas) and return to the original writing line.

The ratchet release also makes it possible to draw vertical lines on a page. After releasing, place the point of a ball-point pen at the printing point (or in a hole near the printing point on some machines) and roll the platen. Practice drawing columns.

Typing Mathematical Equations and Chemical Formulas

To typewrite H_2O

    1. Strike H.
    2. Release the ratchet and turn the roller up slightly.
    3. Strike 2.
    4. Return ratchet release to its original position.
    5. Roll the platen back toward you until it clicks.
    6. Type O.

To typewrite $x^2 + y^2 = 108$

To type the **exponents** (the raised numbers), use the ratchet release and **roll** the cylinder **toward you** slightly. (If you should have several formulas on the same line, you can leave blank spaces for the exponents; then backspace, release the ratchet, and type in all the exponents at once.) Always remember to reengage the ratchet and click the roller to its original position.

To typewrite degrees after a figure, use a small raised o.

```
0° Centigrade = 32° Fahrenheit.
```

Follow the same method as typing exponents.

If you have an electronic typewriter, your machine may have half-line spacing on the gauge. You can roll the platen $\frac{1}{2}$ line toward you or away from you to type exponents or chemical formulas.

Using Variable Line Spacer

By pressing in the end of the left knob of the roller and turning the roller either up or toward you, you can establish a new writing line. This is especially useful for typing on lines—for checks, invoices, and other business forms.

It will take a little practice to judge exactly how to adjust the roller to type on lines with your own machine. The line should have the same relation to the typing as the underscore does—there should be a slight space between.

(a) On a sheet of lined paper, using the variable line spacer, type the underscore. The underscore should cover the line. Make adjustments until you can repeatedly type the underscore on several lines.

(b) Type your name on three successive lines. Observe the relation of the line to the printing indicator.

(c) Type the following paragraph on lined paper.

Both the ratchet release and the variable line spacer disengage the line-spacing mechanism. The variable line spacer establishes a new line of writing. The ratchet release does *not* establish a new line of writing. When it is back in position, the original writing line clicks into place.

(d) Use the variable line spacer for typing a double underscore. Move the roller up the slightest amount for the second underscore. If your machine has a repeat key, use it. (Lock the shift key, strike the underscore once and press the repeat key for the length of the underscore.)

Type this:

<u>We can now establish that the above report is accurate.</u>

Double spacing

Self-Testing Work

Type the following:

Although the temperature today is 90°, it is 75° indoors.

The most commonly known chemical formula is H_2O, water.

Do you know these formulas: H_2SO_4, CO_2?

$4^2 + 5^2 + 8^2 = x$.

Do not underline the subtotal, but underscore the <u>total</u>.

Normal body temperature is 98.6°.

Type these paragraphs.

SOME TIPS FOR TYPING CHECKS

Checks should be typed perfectly. There should be no corrections or alterations.

Check the spelling of the name to whom the check is addressed before typing.

Type the figures close to the dollar sign so that no number can be squeezed between.

Start typing the amount spelled out close to the left so that nothing can be inserted, and type hyphens to fill in the empty space to the word DOLLARS.
$78.50 is spelled out Seventy-eight and 50/100-------
$512.36 is Five Hundred Twelve and 36/100-----------
$6500.00 is Six Thousand Five Hundred and 00/100----
The signature is, of course, handwritten in ink.

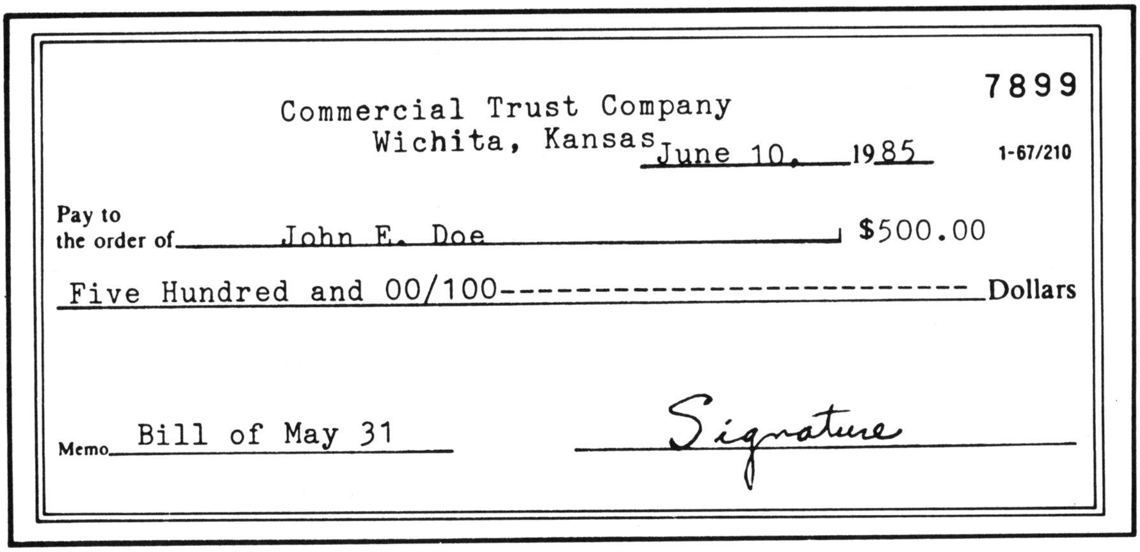

```
+------------------------------------------------------------+
|  +-------------------------------------------------------+ |
|  |                                             7899      | |
|  |          Commercial Trust Company                     | |
|  |             Wichita, Kansas June 10,  19 85  1-67/210 | |
|  | Pay to                                                | |
|  | the order of____John E. Doe_____ $500.00   | |
|  | Five Hundred and 00/100-----------------------Dollars | |
|  |                                                       | |
|  |                                                       | |
|  | Memo__Bill of May 31____    ___Signature_____ | |
|  +-------------------------------------------------------+ |
+------------------------------------------------------------+
```

Fig. 49

TYPING ON PRINTED BUSINESS FORMS

If you must fill in similar forms frequently, it saves time to use one form as a model for reference. You may need to type invoices, statements, order forms, receipts, or promissory notes. You should have a model for each form.

To make a model:

1. Insert the blank form in the typewriter at the paper guide with the left edge at 0.
2. Clear margins and tab stops.
3. Space to the point on the form where the item closest to the left edge will be typed. At this spot on the form, write the number for the left margin.
4. Space to each point on the form where an item such as the date, name, a description, or a column of figures is to be typed. At that point on the form, write the number of the tab stop to be set.

CROSS & SUTTER
Dealers in Chinaware
6589 Main Street
Charlottesville, Virginia 22902

Invoice No. x

x   (Date)

SOLD TO ___x_____

_____

_____

Terms:	x	Shipped via	x			
Quantity	Description		Unit price		Amount	
x	x		x	x	x	x

Fig. 50

Whenever a similar form must be filled in, just set the left margin and tab stops according to the numbers noted on the model. There is no need for a right margin stop.

Vertical lines for listing dollars and cents on forms like deposit slips, invoices, and statements eliminate the need to type the dollar sign or the decimal.

If the invoice on p. 170 were a form you were using, you would place the left margin stop for the *x* under "Quantity." Although there are ten *x*'s for tab stops, you would need to set only five. The same tab stop can be used for more than one item. Wherever an *x* appears, write the number for the tab stop on the model form.

Typing on Index Cards or Labels

If your machine has a card holder, insert the card or label from the front of the platen. Hold it in place with the small rollers.

If your machine does not have a card holder, create a holder by making a narrow pleat across on a regular-size paper. Insert the paper in the typewriter so that the pleat is open at the top, just above the writing line. Insert the card or label in the pleat from the front. Adjust the rollers. Roll the cylinder toward you. The card or label will be anchored for typing. As you remove one card, another can be inserted.

If it is necessary to type close to the bottom edge of a paper, insert the bottom end of the paper in the pleat, as you do a card. You can then type to within a quarter-inch of the bottom.

CALCULATING MARGINS FOR PAPER OF VARIOUS WIDTHS

A. Insert paper with left edge at 0. Note the number on the scale for the right edge.

B. Decide on your left margin: 1″, 1½″, or 2″. With pica 1″ = 10; 1½″ = 15; 2″ = 20. (With elite 1″ = 12; 1½″ = 18; 2″ = 24.)

C. Subtract the number of the left margin from the number of the right edge of the paper. The remainder is the number of the right margin.

D. Set the right margin.

ADDITIONAL FEATURES ON SOME ELECTRONIC TYPEWRITERS

Can be connected to a computer and act as a printer for multiple letters, mailing lists, and calculations.

Choice of triple pitch: 10, 12, 15.

Automatic RETURN programmed within five spaces of the margin.

Automatic centering.

Display of typed material before printing.

Various type faces easily changed.

Symbols for foreign languages.

Automatic underscore.

Decimal tab for statistical typing. Automatically aligns numbers by their decimal points.

Right-margin justification.

Simultaneous text typing and storage.

Repeat action for all keys.

Vertical advancement key.

Preestablished settings for margins and tab stops.
Automatic spelling correction.

When buying a machine decide which, if any, of these features are important to you. Compare machines. Study the operating manuals. Test the keyboard for over sensitivity.

Now that you have completed this course of study, you have full mastery of the keyboard and the machine. Should you decide to operate a word processor or a computer, you have the basic skill on which to build.

Your speed will improve with typing. However, if you have set a goal of a definite speed, time yourself on several five-minute timings a day. You can use the timed copy in this book or you can type from magazine articles or books. To calculate speed, as you have learned, add the number of words in three lines, divide by three, and multiply by the number of lines. This will give you the number of words you typed in five minutes. Always practice corrections. If a particular letter troubles you, practice the lesson that introduces that letter.

You have a very valuable skill. Good luck!

A Word About Word Processors and Computers

The "QWERTY" keyboard system, so named because the letters on the keyboard from the top left spell q-w-e-r-t-y, was adopted on manual typewriters early in the development of the typewriter and has been used on all manual, electric, and electronic machines ever since. Nearly all word processors and computers have this same arrangement of keys, so once you have mastered touch typing, you can easily apply your skills to the computer keyboard. If you know how to touch-type, your fingers will move easily over the keyboard once you have adjusted to the different feel of the keys.

When you type on a word processor or computer, you are entering words into the system. But words made up of letters are not the only characters you enter into the system. You have to tell the system what to do with the words you are generating: You issue these commands to the computer system also by pressing a single key.

If you want to learn more about keyboarding on word processors or computers, you might want to consult *Word Processing Made Simple* and *Computer Typing Made Simple* (both written by Betty and Warner A. Hutchinson and published by Doubleday & Company, Inc.), which fully explain the different techniques and additional keys.